God Wants You Healed

Eighteen Ways God Will Heal You

Walt Straughan

Walt Straughan Ministries

Walt Straughan Ministries
59 Rosebud Lane
Staunton, VA 24401
Phone 540-337-5123

Unless otherwise indicated, all scriptural quotations are taken from the King James Version of the Bible.

First Printing 1999

ISBN 0-9627353-4-5

In the U.S.A. write:

Walt Straughan Ministries
59 Rosebud Lane
Staunton, VA 24401
Phone 540-337-5123

OR

~~P. O. Box 1489~~
~~Mechanicsville, MD 20659~~

Speaking Engagements
or
Teaching Seminars

Walt Straughan is available for seminar and speaking engagements throughout the year for churches, conferences, and special meetings.

Please contact:

Walt Straughan Ministries
59 Rosebud Lane
Staunton, VA 24401
Phone 540-337-5123

Table of Contents

Introduction

Would you like to be healed? Do you know anyone who needs healing? If the answer to either one of these questions is yes, then this book is written for you.

God has provided healing for His children today. He wants us to be healed and healthy, and He wants us to walk in divine health. The provision to live in divine health comes from believing and acting upon the knowledge you receive from the Word of God, and by the power of the Holy Spirit.

When Adam sinned in the Garden of Eden he died spiritually. God told him if he ate from the tree of the knowledge of good and evil that he would die. Well, he ate the fruit from the tree, but he didn't immediately die physically. Adam lived approximately 930 years after he ate the fruit. However, he did die spiritually and sin entered into him when his spirit man died. This happened when the serpent deceived Adam through Eve and caused Adam to disobey God. The authority God had given Adam was then transferred to Satan by this sin of disobedience, and Satan became the god of this world's system (II Corinthians 4:4).

When Satan became the god of this world, he brought everything that steals, kills and destroys with him (John 10:10). As a result, destructive things began to manifest themselves such as sickness and disease. Man was made to live forever before Adam sinned, but spiritual death brought on physical death. Physical death should consist of man growing old, wearing out, dying and going on to heaven. But most Christian's die from some type of sickness or disease, not experiencing the longevity of life promised in God's Word. This should not be happening in the body of Christ. Not only should we die free from sickness or disease, but we should also know in advance before we die (Psalms 90 and 91), because the Holy Spirit will show us things to come (John 16:13).

When sin entered into man, death entered into his bloodstream. Even though it took Satan about 930 years to kill Adam, that was relatively a short period of time because Adam was supposed to live forever. Before the flood of Noah's day, most of the Old Testament patriarchs lived to be over 900 years old. One thousand years after the flood, man was only living to be 120 years old. From Noah to Moses, 1,000 years in time, man went from living for 900 years to 120 years on earth because of the sin passed down from Adam. Since that time, the life span of man has been reduced to a range of 70 to 90 years of age, mostly because of sickness.

The first healing mentioned in the Bible is found in Genesis 20:17, "So Abraham prayed unto God: and God healed Abimelech, and his wife, and his maidservants; and they bare children." It took sickness a few thousand years to gain momentum in the human race before it began to kill the majority of the people.

After Adam's fall in the Garden of Eden, God made a covenant with him that covered every provision for man's needs, including physical healing. God kept making covenants with men such as Noah, Abraham, Moses, and David. He also made a New Covenant that believers today live under. In these covenants, God always provided healing for the body and peace for the mind. In each covenant, God has a part that He does and man has his part to perform. If we will follow the instructions that God gave us in His Word, we will always receive our healing and deliverance.

God has always done what He said He would do for us in these covenants, and it is up to us to do our part. God is always waiting on us to line ourselves up with His Word, which is His covenant. The promises of God pertaining to healing show us that the provision was made by Christ's sacrifice (...by whose stripes [Jesus] ye were healed--I Peter 2:24). We just need to receive what has already been provided for us. These promises of healing are always past tense. When we act on the promise of healing by faith, we will always receive our healing.

During Jesus' three and one-half years of ministry on earth, He said, "...Verily, verily, I say unto you, The Son can do nothing of himself, but what he seeth the Father do: for what things soever he doeth, these also doeth the Son likewise" (John 5:19). Jesus said that everything He did, He saw His Father do it first. The majority of Jesus' earthly ministry was healing and delivering the sick. Jesus healed every person who came to Him for healing no matter what was wrong with them. He never told anyone that they were too sick for Him to heal them. He healed the lame, dumb, blind, and maimed. He healed every sickness of those who came to Him (Matthew 15:30-31). If you have ever noticed, Jesus healed everyone who came to Him for healing in all the four Gospels. However, every sick person around Him was not necessarily healed just because they were in the area.

This same thing takes place today in churches that believe in healing, because everyone who is sick in the church is not automatically healed. The sick person needs to come to God and ask, believing God for his or her healing. Then and only then can the power of the Holy Spirit produce a healing in the body. We are instructed to believe the Word of God and to not doubt. If we will do that, we will always receive our healing.

We are held responsible for our mind and body (Romans 12:1-2). We are instructed to renew our mind with the Word of God and to present our body as a living sacrifice to God. Then God holds us accountable for everything we have knowledge of concerning His Word and also in the natural realm. The Bible says in I John 3:21, "...if our hearts condemn us not, then have we confidence (faith) toward God." We can never operate in faith if our heart is condemning us or telling us that we are doing something wrong. If we know that what we are doing doesn't agree with the Word of God, we can't stay in faith and believe God for the answer. We will have to make an adjustment with our attitude before we can believe God for the answer.

One area the body of Christ has a major problem in is in the area of diet and nutrition. We act like we can eat anything we want to eat and still just exercise faith to stay healthy. But this is not working very well in the Church, because believers in the Church are almost as sick as people in the world. After teaching divine healing and praying for the sick for over 20 years, I know that we can't override our bad diet with our faith.

The diet of the western world is filled with saturated fats, cholesterol, sugar, and different types of chemicals, which cause all kinds of sicknesses and diseases. Even the water we drink has chemicals added to it that cause all kinds of sickness. All of these fats, chemicals and drugs have a negative reaction in our body. They cause different kinds of cancer, diabetes, heart problems, and all types of sicknesses and diseases.

If you are working with someone who has diabetes, you will probably have to get him to change his diet before he can receive his healing and keep it over a long period of time. I have never worked with anyone who had diabetes that was not eventually healed. It usually takes a little time, but if they will believe the Word of God and speak to the mountain of diabetes it will have to leave them.

Many who are healed of diabetes may have to monitor their diet the rest of their lives. It will be necessary for them to study nutrition until they have the knowledge needed to eat proper foods. Even as Christians, the older we get, the more we should check our diets.

We need to eat as much natural food as possible every day, and eliminate saturated fats, processed foods, sugar, and chemicals as much as possible. We should also eat as many salads, fruits and vegetables as possible each day. God programmed healing in our minds and bodies when He made us, and if we will give the body a chance, it will heal itself.

When a doctor gives someone medication, the medication doesn't heal the person, but sometimes it helps the body to heal itself. We need to feed the cells in our bodies through oxygen, enzymes, vitamins, minerals, and filtered water every day. This can be accomplished by eating live foods (salads, fruits and vegetables) and by breathing deeply every day for 30 minutes or more through aerobic exercise.

Some experts have said that if we would change our eating habits and switch our diets to natural foods that 90 percent of all of our major sicknesses would begin to disappear in six months. That would indicate that 90 percent of all cancers, heart problems, strokes, diabetes, and other sicknesses would disappear from society. The message this relays to us is that we are eating ourselves into sickness by not taking the responsibility for the food we are eating. Ninety percent of the sickness the Church is praying about could be caused by bad eating habits.

We need to check on what we are going to eat before we eat it. If we can't sanctify and bless our food with faith and prayer, then we should not eat it. In America we don't have trouble with starvation, but we do have a problem with gluttony. We are bringing all kinds of sicknesses and diseases upon ourselves by overeating. We are eating ourselves to death with our high fat, cholesterol, sugar, and chemical diet.

If our hearts condemn us because of the food we are eating, we can't bless and sanctify it by faith and prayer before we eat it (I John 3:21). Under these conditions God can't protect us from the consequences of eating bad food. It is almost impossible to bless food if you know it is bad for you!

Concerning divine healing, the New Testament informs born again Christians that God has already healed them (I Peter 2:24). It is one thing to read that promise in the Bible, but it is another thing to receive healing in our bodies, especially if we have a very serious sickness. Sometimes when we get sick, we go to the Bible and see where God is telling us we are healed; but the doctors, our minds, bodies, relatives, and everybody else could be saying we are sick.

Well, we have to make a decision as to whom we are going to believe. Are we going to believe God or what everyone else is saying, and that includes our mind and body? Our bodies will tell us we are sick through symptoms. They are designed this way to warn us if something is not working correctly. We should not ignore what our mind or body is saying to us with the symptoms of sickness. This is how we know something is wrong.

The Bible doesn't tell us to ignore the devil. It tells us to resist him and he will flee from us in James 4:7. God's Word operates on a higher level than the sickness in our bodies. God's Word is Spirit and truth, and it will override the sickness and drive it out. However, we have to put the Word of God inside of us until it replaces the sickness. Until the Word has changed our thoughts, emotions and feelings, it is not in our hearts nor has it become a part of us.

We will need to read and meditate on the Word of God, and pray until God our Father can make the healing promises a part of us. Always remember that anything we ask God for, we have to receive. Sometimes it takes time to renew our minds with the Word of God so that we can receive our answer. The Word of God and the Spirit of God (Holy Spirit) will remove sickness from our body and bring healing to every area of our lives. But, we have to make the final decision to receive and accept God's promises over any other report.

Look over these 18 ways to receive healing and make a decision as to which method you are going to use to receive your healing. Make sure you spend quality time in prayer and waiting on the Lord. Then ask the Holy Spirit to lead and guide you as you make this decision. Take the outline from this book and the Word of God pertaining to these different ways you will be using to receive your healing and memorize them. Meditate on the Word of God until it becomes a part of you. Then begin to act on God's Word until you are healed. I believe in being healed and not sick. Use any of these 18 ways to receive your healing anytime you get sick.

My Prayer For You: Heavenly Father, I ask You to save, heal, deliver, and set free each and every one who reads this book in their spirit, soul and body in the name of Jesus. I cover them with the blood of Jesus and pray God's promises on them and their families. I speak healing and deliverance in every area of their lives in the name of Jesus. Fill them with your knowledge, wisdom, grace, and make your Word more real to them each day. Pour your blessings upon them in the name of Jesus!

Chapter 1

Healing in the Word of God

My son, attend to my words; incline thine ear unto my sayings. Let them not depart from thine eyes; keep them in the midst of thine heart. For they are life unto those that find them, and health (healing, medicine) to all their flesh.

Proverbs 4:20-22

Psalm 107:20
He sent his word, and healed them (me), and delivered them (me) from their (my) destructions.

I Peter 2:24
Who his own self (Jesus) bare our sins in his own body on the tree, that we, being dead to sins, should live unto righteousness: by whose (Jesus') stripes ye were (I was) healed.

Matthew 8:17
That it might be fulfilled which was spoken by
Esaias the prophet, saying, Himself (Jesus) took
our infirmities, and bare our (my) sicknesses.

There is healing and health in the Word of God. God tells us in Psalm 107:20 that He sent His Word and healed us. We can read the Bible, which is God's Word, for years and never realize it will heal us unless we are looking for healing or unless someone informs us that there is healing in God's Word. Even after this happens, the Holy Spirit has to give us a revelation as to what the Word is saying about healing to make it real to us. We can go for years never realizing that believing and acting on the Word of God can heal, deliver and set us free from all sickness.

Under the Old Testament, God made provisions for His people to walk in divine health. As long as they obeyed His commandments and followed them, they would stay healthy. When God brought the nation of Israel out of Egypt after being in slavery and bondage for 400 years, there was not one who was sick (Psalm 105:37)! There were 600,000 men plus the women and children, which most Bible scholars believe to be over two million people, and there was not one feeble or sick person among them.

God healed every one of them no matter how sick or weak they were before He brought them out of Egypt. In Exodus 15:26 God said if they would diligently listen to His voice, and do that which was right in His sight, and give ear to His commandments, and keep His statutes, then

He would be the Lord that would heal them and keep them healthy. As long as they walked in line with His Word and listened to His voice they stayed healed and healthy.

Throughout the Old Testament, God told His people over and over that He would keep them healed and healthy if they would listen to Him and obey His Word. The same principle applies today for us under the New Covenant. Peter through the inspiration of the Holy Spirit said in I Peter 2:24 that by His (Jesus') stripes we were healed. You might be able to believe that statement as a Christian if you are not sick and if you don't pray for those who are sick.

However, if there is pressure on you because of a sickness in your own body or because of someone else's sickness, then sometimes it becomes a different story. You will have to know what the Bible has to say about healing before you can stand on the Word and believe God for your healing or anyone else's. When you are praying for the sick, most of the time, the only thing you are basing your prayers on is what the Word of God says about healing. It is very important to know the chapter and verse that supports what God has already said and done about healing and health for the believer.

When I got sick several years ago and began to study God's Word on healing, the most amazing thing I found in the Word was that God had already healed me as far as His Word was concerned. At first I couldn't understand or believe what the Bible was saying along this line. After a few weeks of Bible study and meditation in the Word, I decided to make a decision to believe God's Word and not what everyone else was saying, and that included the people in the church I was attending. After making that decision, it enabled me to accept God's Word and receive healing for my body.

I teach how to receive healing through 18 different ways from our heavenly Father. **All 18 ways start and end with the Word of God**. Sickness and disease started in the human race when Adam and Eve sinned in the Garden of Eden. More and more sicknesses and diseases are coming upon mankind each day. There are so many sicknesses that the doctors cannot even help us with because there is no medication to help cure these diseases.

Where are they coming from? John 10:10 tells us where sickness and disease come from and who puts sickness on us. Satan is the originator of all sickness. Always remember that sickness and disease come from the kingdom of darkness, and they are sent to steal, kill and destroy the human race. You can divide everything in life that comes at you with John 10:10, because it either steals, kills or destroys--or it brings abundant life. If it brings abundant life, then it is from God, your Father, and comes from the kingdom of light. If it steals, kills or destroys it is from Satan, and it comes from the kingdom of darkness.

One of Satan's jobs is to steal your health by putting sickness on you. You have to understand this and make a decision as to what you will do about any sickness or disease that attacks your body.

The decision is yours to make concerning sickness. You make the final decision as to whether or not you will walk in divine health. **The first step on your part is to agree with the Word of God. The second step is to resist the sickness with the name of Jesus.**

Spend time each day reading and meditating on the Word of God. This will keep your faith strong. The more you do this, the stronger your faith will become in the area of your meditation. If you need healing in your body, don't spend all your time studying and meditating on the subject of the end times! Spend most of your time reading and meditating on healing scriptures. It will help you to mark all the healing scriptures in your Bible and go through them each day.

Also, you will need to spend time before God's throne and in His presence each day in prayer (Hebrews 4:16). It is necessary to pray (speak out) and believe the promises you are reading in God's Word. Believing on and releasing faith in the Word of God is something we need to do day and night if we are sick. You may need to read your confessions out loud three to four times a day, just like you need to take doses of medicine that often.

The Bible instructs us to resist the devil so he will flee from us in James 4:7. If we didn't know that the Bible said this, the devil could kill us with a sickness, and we would blame God for it. In fact, many pastors and most churches blame God for all sickness today, but that does not agree with what the Bible teaches. In I Timothy 6:12, the Word of God instructs us to fight the good fight of faith. This verse is letting us know that to resist the devil (sickness and disease) will require a fight.

The Bible calls it a good fight of faith because we always win if we don't quit too soon. We have to make a strong decision to resist the sickness until it leaves our bodies and we are completely healed. While we are resisting the problem, the Word and the Kingdom of God are in agreement with us, backing us 100 percent. Unfortunately, we need to be prepared for the fact that the world and most people around us, including a lot of Christians, may not give us much encouragement.

The Bible says in Matthew 8:17 "...Himself (Jesus) took our infirmities, and bare our sicknesses." In I Peter 2:24 it says, "...by whose stripes ye (we) were healed." III John 2 says, "...that thou mayest prosper and be in health." These promises inform us that God has already healed us, and that He desires for us to walk in divine health all the time. If we want to walk in divine health, however, we have to read and meditate on the Word, and pray a certain amount of time each day.

The problems and circumstances surrounding our lives will determine how long we need to spend in the Word and prayer each day. Some will have to spend more time in the Word and less time in prayer or vice versa. If you have a sickness or disease that is killing you, and the doctors can't help you with it, you will probably have to spend most of the hours of each day in prayer and the Word. You will have to spend most of your waking time resisting the sickness in the name of Jesus until it leaves.

If you are concerned about false doctrines or what the Bible says about any subject, including healing, always make sure that you have more than one promise or Bible verse for that subject. There are hundreds and hundreds of verses in the Bible on the subject of healing. Put some of them on 3 X 5 cards and memorize them. You need to get the Word inside of you, in your heart, until it becomes a part of your life.

In Hebrews 4:12 the Word of God tells us, "the word of God is quick, and powerful, and sharper than any two-edged sword, piercing even to the dividing asunder of soul and spirit, and of the joints and marrow, and is a discerner of the thoughts and intents of the heart." This Word will cut cancer, Aids, lupus, diabetes, tumors, strokes, arthritis, and all sicknesses and diseases out of our bodies. The Word will separate our joints from our bone marrow. Yes, this Word, on our lips, will remove anything from our body that steals, kills or destroys.

We are the ones that have to make sure we put this healing Word of God inside our hearts. We have to believe the Word of God over all reports, and this includes our doctor's report, no matter how much you like and appreciate him or her. The Word has to be stronger inside of your heart than your five senses: seeing, hearing, feeling, tasting, and smelling. We will need to make a decision to put the Word first place in our lives. This means over all sicknesses or diseases that would be in your bodies.

The Word will change our thought patterns and bring them into agreement with God's Word. We will receive the mind of Christ as we read, meditate and speak the Word of God. It will take away all worry, anxiety and fear from our lives. It will make us more than conquerors through Christ Jesus.

If you are worried because of a doctor's report or because of the symptoms in your body, you haven't renewed your mind with God's Word. Worry can prevent you from receiving your healing. If you are worried or if there is any problem with your thought life, it will be necessary for you to spend more time renewing your mind with the Word by reading and meditating on it. Keep doing this until your thoughts are positive and in agreement with the Word of God. This will remove your worries and put you into a position to receive your healing.

Steps for Receiving Healing from God's Word:
1.   Have at lease two verses or promises from the Bible for your healing.
2.   Memorize and meditate on the scriptures until they have become a part of you. Put them in your heart.
3.   Make a decision to act on the Word of God concerning your healing.
4.   Release faith by confessing the Word of God and by acting on the Word.

5. Thank, praise and worship God until you have your answer.

Pray this prayer: Heavenly Father, I ask you to open my heart and fill it with your Word. Help me to understand and comprehend your Word, and to make it a part of my life in the name of Jesus. I receive the anointing from the Word of God into my mind and body to heal, deliver and set me free from all sickness, disease, bondage, and weakness in the name of Jesus. Body, by Jesus' stripes you are healed.

Chapter 2

Healing Through Praying in Jesus' Name

And in that day ye shall ask me nothing. Verily, verily, I say unto you, Whatsoever ye shall ask the Father in my name, he will give it you. Hitherto have ye asked nothing in my name: ask, and ye shall receive, that your joy may be full.

John 16:23-24

John 15:16
Ye have not chosen me, but I have chosen you, and ordained you, that ye should go and bring forth fruit, and that your fruit should remain: that whatsoever ye shall ask of the Father in my name, he may give it you.

We can ask God our Father for healing in the name of Jesus with a simple child-like faith and receive healing for any sickness or disease. We will need to boldly stand on God's Word until our healing manifests itself. Under the New Testament, or New Covenant that believers today are living under, if we want to go to God our Father, we have to go through our intercessor, the Lord Jesus Christ. We should make our prayers and petitions to our Father in the name of Jesus. We don't ask for healing from our Father in the name of the Father, Son and Holy Ghost. This is not the scriptural way to pray under the New Testament. We should always go to our Father in Jesus' name. When we are thanking, praising or worshiping our heavenly Father, it should always be done in the name of Jesus.

> ***Sample prayer***   Heavenly Father, I ask you for
> _____Your Petition_____ in the name of Jesus.

Under the Old Covenant, God's covenant people had to go through a priest, king or prophet to get to God. When someone committed a sin, they had to bring an animal to the temple, and the priest would kill it and take the blood of the animal and sprinkle it on the altar. The blood would be an atonement or covering for their sin. Every time someone wanted to go to God for any reason under the Mosaic Covenant, they had to go through the priest. Under the New Covenant, which applies to Christians, we can go directly to God our Father through the name of Jesus.

In Ephesians 5:20, the Word instructs us to give thanks to God in the name of Jesus. We are told to thank God for everything and to thank Him continually. Thanksgiving should be on our lips all the time, but the only way we can reach God with our thanksgiving is in the name of Jesus.

Hebrews 13:15 says, "...offer the sacrifice of praise to God continually, that is, the fruit of our lips giving thanks to his name." When we praise God for the things we have and for the things we need, it should be done in the name of Jesus. All praise to the Father should be done in the name of Jesus.

When we worship our Father, which is something we should do each day, we should worship Him in the name of Jesus. In Colossians 3:17 we are instructed to do everything in the name of Jesus, and this includes worshiping our heavenly Father. This worship should flow out of our spirits to our Father in the name of Jesus.

Study and meditate in the Word of God on the subject of the name of Jesus, until you build faith in your heart in His name. Every time you speak the phrase "in the name of Jesus," you should be releasing faith from your heart, because you know that you know, that the name "Jesus" is above every name in heaven, on earth, and in Hell (Philippians 2:9-11).

When you speak the name of Jesus and pray in line with God's Word, your prayers will always be answered. The most important name that you will ever speak is the name of Jesus. Begin to thank and praise Jesus for giving you His powerful name to use against your adversary while you are living on this earth.

Steps for Praying to God in Jesus' Name:

1. Meditate on the scriptures that instruct us on how to ask in Jesus' name.
2. Always ask for your petitions from the Father in the name of Jesus.
3. Every time you go to God, go in Jesus' name.
4. Thank, praise and worship God in Jesus' name until you have your answer.

Chapter 3

Healing Through the Prayer of Faith or Petition

And all things, whatsoever ye shall ask in prayer, believing, ye shall receive.

Matthew 21:22

Mark 11:23-24
For verily I say unto you, That whosoever shall say unto this mountain, Be thou removed, and be thou cast into the sea; and shall not doubt in his heart, but shall believe that those things which he saith shall come to pass; he shall have whatsoever he saith.
Therefore I say unto you, What things soever ye (you) desire, when ye (you) pray, believe that ye (you) receive them, and ye (you) shall have them.

Receiving healing through the Prayer of Faith or Petition is asking God for something in the name of Jesus. You have to believe in your heart that you have already received the answer to your petition, based on God's Word, before the answer will ever manifest itself in your body. When you finish praying and asking for your healing, you will have to believe you have received by faith until you are completely healed.

We, as believers, cannot be controlled by our five senses which are: feeling, seeing, tasting, smelling, and hearing if we are going to walk and live by faith. We have to live on a higher plain than our five senses. God's Word will have to control our thoughts and this will keep us in faith. The Bible instructs us to walk by faith and not by sight in II Corinthians 5:7. It is not an easy thing to do at times, especially if there is pain in your body or if the doctor has given you a very bad report. God's Word will have to be stronger in your heart than the pressure coming against your five senses in order for you to stay in faith.

The battle is always in the soul realm where your mind is located. The thought patterns in your mind will have to be controlled and brought into agreement with what the Word of God says about healing. In II Corinthians 10:4-5 the Word tells us to cast down all thoughts and imaginations that are contrary to the promises in God's Word. Reading and meditating on healing scriptures, which are God's promises, will keep faith in your heart. As you confess and act on these promises, the power and anointing to heal your body will come through the scriptures and heal you.

Romans 10:17 lets us know where faith comes from and how to increase our faith. This verse informs us that faith comes from God's Word, and that we can increase our faith by reading and hearing the Word of God. Faith and the Word of God is the same thing. They are interchangeable. If you have faith in your heart, you will always have God's Word in your heart. If you have God's Word in your heart, you will always have faith in your heart. You need to spend time each day reading and meditating on God's Word to put faith in your heart.

In Hebrews 11:1 the Word of God tells us that faith is the substance (proof) of things hoped for and the evidence of things not seen. This tells us that as long as we are operating in faith, we have not yet received the answer in the natural. I don't know why the Church has a problem with faith because it is very simple to understand. If we believe by faith we are healed, it means the healing has not yet manifested itself. Once we are healed, we don't need faith to believe for that healing, but we may need to do some things to maintain or hold on to our healing.

As Bible-believing Christians, we should always have things we are believing God for by faith, because the Bible says that without faith it is impossible to please God (Hebrews 11:6).

What is the Prayer of Faith? It is believing in your heart, that what you say with your mouth will come to pass, and saying it. It is acting on the Word of God you have in your heart with your confession and with your actions. In Proverbs 3:5 the Word says, "Trust in the Lord with all thine (your) heart; and lean not unto thine own understanding (your thoughts)." Trusting God is trusting and believing His Word. You cannot trust and believe a man without believing what he says. If his words are not any good, he cannot be trusted. This same rule applies to God. If you can't trust His Word, then you can't believe Him. What God said in the Bible is His Word, and you can put all your trust and belief in that Word. You are walking in faith when you trust God's Word and not your five senses.

In Mark 11:22-26 God gave us an outline for the Prayer of Faith. In verse 22 Jesus told us to "Have faith in God" or "Have the faith of God." If we have this God kind of faith, we will be following the instructions that Jesus gave us in Mark 11:23-26.

In Mark 11:23 He is talking about speaking in faith and not doubting in our hearts. Jesus said to speak to the mountain (cancer, diabetes, lupus, blood pressure, weakness, etc.), and tell it to be removed and cast into the sea (specifically, to leave our bodies and don't come back). He further says to not doubt in our heart (but believe in our heart). We are to believe that those things which we say (confess) shall come to pass--then we shall have whatsoever we say. This verse is instructing us to speak to the sickness and tell it where to go and stay. We should not doubt in our heart, but continue to believe what we are saying will come to pass, and it always will.

In Mark 11:24 Jesus is talking about praying, believing and receiving. He said, "what things (healing, health) soever ye (your name) desire, when ye (your name) pray, believe that ye (your name) receive them (those things you ask for), and ye (your name) shall have them." The word "shall" doesn't mean that you already have them, it means what it says, and that is, that you shall have them. The word "shall" is future. You shall have the answer (healing) after you pray and believe you have received it by faith.

This verse is informing us that we can have anything God has provided for us if we will believe we have already received it when we pray. We have to believe we received first and then we will have it second. The believing always comes before we can receive the answer. When we pray the Prayer of Faith, there is always a span of time between the believing we have received and the manifestation of our answer. Sometimes it might be five minutes, five hours, five days, or longer. It often depends on the sickness and the circumstances surrounding it. But, remember, **healing will always come if we will stand on God's Word**.

In Mark 11:25-26 we are told to forgive if we have aught (anything) against anybody. This means, before we pray, we need to get rid of all strife, hate, resentment, animosity, or dislike that we have against anyone. If we don't do this, the devil can hinder or stop our prayers from being answered. Jesus told us to love one another in John 13:34. We are supposed to love each other by faith just because the Word instructs us to love one another. We don't love people just because we feel like it. It's not based on feelings, it's based on what Jesus told us to do. We need to make a decision to get rid of all strife and ask the Holy

Spirit to love them through us. **If we will do this, the devil can't stop us from receiving the answers to our prayers.**

Jesus spoke these verses in Mark 11:22-26 all at one time. He didn't give us Mark 11:22-23 one day and come back two weeks later and give us the rest of these verses from Mark 11:24-26. All five of these verses contain the God kind of faith and the Prayer of Faith or Petition. Verse 23 is telling us to say and verse 24 is telling us to pray. You can't pray without saying, and you can't say without praying, if you are asking God for something.

I am convinced that God wants us to pray out loud if we can, but if we can't pray out loud, we can pray on the inside very loudly at times. We can never pray and ask for something according to Mark 11:24 and believe we have received what we have asked for, and be confessing something different. According to Mark 11:23, our confession will always have to agree with what we have prayed for if we want to receive the answer to our prayer. Our confession (what we are saying) always has to agree with what we have asked for in the Prayer of Faith before we can receive the answer to our prayer with our faith.

Now, how does this confession and prayer work together? Look at Mark 11:24. It says, "believe that ye receive them, and ye shall have them." Ninety-eight percent of the time when you pray the Prayer of Faith or Petition, the answer to your prayer will not be instant. In fact, most Prayers of Faith that have been prayed over the years have never been answered instantly, and I don't think they ever will be. It may take only a few moments to receive the answer, but remember even that is not instant.

If it takes a while for the answer to manifest itself, what do you do in the meantime? In Mark 11:24, where it says, "And ye shall have them," put Mark 11:23 in the place of the word "and." From that point of time do what Mark 11:23 instructs you to do. Speak to the mountain (sickness, disease) telling it to leave your body and not return. You can do this as many times and as long as you would like to and still be in faith. Every time you speak to the sickness, you are releasing faith against the mountain until it leaves. Make sure while you are speaking to the mountain that you are believing you have already received the answer to your prayer or petition.

Remember, just because you believe something, it doesn't mean that you will receive anything from what you believe. For example, if you had a bicycle, you could believe that if you got on that bicycle and rode two miles down the road, you would come to a store. The store is two miles down the road and the bicycle will take you there, but until you take what you believe and put it into action, you will never get the end result (get to the store).

This is a natural law that works every time. We know this natural law, and we don't have any problem operating in it. Believers need to realize that in the spiritual realm, we have spiritual laws that work the same way. We have to take the Word of God (what we believe), and **act on it**. The action is our faith at work, and this is what brings the answer.

There are two things that we have to do to get our faith to work for us. We have to use these two procedures to get results every time we pray the Prayer of Faith. These two things are our confession and some type of physical action. We need to be confessing the Word by speaking to the mountain (sickness) and telling it where to go and stay. But we also need to put some type of physical action into motion as to what we believe. Make sure you have your confession and actions moving in line with God's Word. If you don't know what type of action to apply to the Word and to the prayer, you will have to pray and ask the Holy Spirit to show you what to do. Get in your prayer closet and stay there until you have your answer.

Let's take a look at one of the lowest levels of faith in the New Testament. In John 20:24-29, we see the disciple Thomas whom Jesus called "faithless." This name was given to him after Jesus was raised from the dead. Jesus had first appeared to His disciples at a time when Thomas was not with them. When the disciples told Thomas that Jesus had appeared to them, Thomas said, "Except I shall see in his hands the print of the nails, and put my finger into the print of the nails, and thrust my hand into his side, I will not believe."

Eight days later, Jesus appeared to the disciples again and this time Thomas was with them. Jesus walked over to Thomas and said "Reach hither thy finger, and behold my hands; and reach hither thy hand, and thrust it into my side: and be not faithless, but believing" (John 20:27). Jesus called Thomas faithless because he would only believe what he could see and feel. Jesus will also call you and I faithless if we only believe what our five senses tell us. We have to believe the Word of God above what our five senses are saying to us. This is what the Bible calls walking by faith and not by sight.

One of the highest levels of faith found in the Bible was that of Abraham. Abraham was around 100 years old and Sarah was 90 years old at the time. They were both past childbearing age, but God had given Abraham a promise of a seed, which was a son (Genesis 15:4-5, Romans 4:16-20). Abraham finally reached a point in his life when he really began to believe God's Word. In Romans chapter four, it tells us that Abraham was not weak in faith, but strong in faith because he considered not his own body that was dead (couldn't reproduce) because he was 100 years old. He neither considered the deadness of Sarah's womb because she was 90 years old. In verse 20 it says, "He staggered not at the promise of God through unbelief; but was strong in faith, giving glory to God." He was convinced that what God said, He would do.

Once Abraham reached this level of faith, he could believe God for a son. If you will notice, he staggered not at the promise of God. Sometimes we look at the promise of God and it looks so impossible that we stagger with doubt and unbelief. But if we are going to believe the promise of healing, we have to be persuaded that God will do what His Word tells us He will do. If we will accept and believe God's Word, we will have strong faith, and we will always receive the answer (healing) to our Prayer of Faith or Petition.

Steps to Receiving Through the Prayer of Faith or Petition:

1. Have two promises from God's Word (chapter and verse) on your healing.
2. Make a decision to believe God's Word. Pray and ask for whatever you need.
3. Get rid of all strife, hate, worry, anxiety, and resentment.
4. Speak to the sickness, and tell it where to go (leave your body) and stay (don't come back) until you have your answer.
5. Thank, praise and worship God, your Father, every day for your healing by faith.

Chapter 4

Healing Through Using the Name of Jesus

And whatsoever ye shall ask in my name, that will I do, that the Father may be glorified in the Son.
If ye shall ask any thing in my name, I will do it.

John 14:13-14

Philippians 2:9-10
Wherefore God also hath highly exalted him, and given him a name which is above every name.
That at the name of Jesus every knee should bow, of things in heaven, and things in earth, and things under the earth (hell).

Colossians 3:17
And whatsoever ye do in word or deed, do all in the name of the Lord Jesus, giving thanks to God and the Father by him.

There are two ways in which we can use the name of Jesus in the Body of Christ. One way is praying to God the Father in the name of Jesus. The other way is using the name of Jesus against our adversary, Satan, and his kingdom of darkness. Here we are going to discuss how to use the name of Jesus against our adversary which includes anything that kills, steals or destroys (John 10:10).

Matthew 1:21 informs us that the name of Jesus means Saviour. The name Christ means anointed one. In Mark 16:15-18 the Bible instructs us to take the name of Jesus and cast out devils, speak with new tongues, and to lay hands on the sick, and they shall recover. The name of Jesus has to have more power in it than demons, sickness, disease, weakness, pain, and everything else that attacks mankind.

In Philippians 2:8-10 the Holy Spirit tells us that God gave Jesus a name above every name in heaven, earth and hell. The only way we can have access to our Father is through the name of Jesus. The only way to cast out demons or heal the sick is in that mighty name of Jesus.

In John 14:12-14 Jesus said that we, His Church, would do the works that He did and also do greater works than what He did. How are we going to do these greater works? We are going to take His name (Jesus) and use it against the kingdom of darkness, Satan and his demons, and set free those that are bound with sickness, disease, poverty, lack, and fear. In verse 13 Jesus said, "And whatsoever ye shall ask in My name that will I do, that the Father may be glorified in the Son." In the Greek, the word "ask" in this verse means command, require or demand. So whatever we command, require or demand the kingdom of darkness (which includes sickness) to do, it has to obey us if we believe what we command in Jesus' name.

We have to have faith in the name of Jesus and be bold in using that name. Remember that the name of Jesus takes the place of Jesus physically walking the earth. When we use the name of Jesus against the devil and his cohorts it is the same as Jesus speaking to them. We are not demanding that God should do anything, but we are demanding that the devil take his hands off the ones we are praying for and off of us.

In Acts chapter three Peter and John went up to the temple to pray at three o'clock in the afternoon. At the gate called Beautiful there was a lame man who was laid there each day to beg for money. He had been crippled from birth. Peter said to the lame man, "Silver and gold have I none; but such as I have give I thee: In the name of Jesus Christ of Nazareth rise up and walk." Peter grabbed the man by his right hand and lifted him up, and immediately his feet and anklebones were healed. He started leaping, walking and praising God.

This healing occurred because Peter knew how to take the name of Jesus and speak a command to the lame man, raising him up and getting him healed. Notice that Peter didn't ask God to do anything. He took the name of Jesus and used it against the sickness. Acts 3:16 explains what happened: "And his name (Jesus) through faith in his name (Jesus) hath made this man strong, whom ye see and know: yea, the faith which is by him hath given him (the lame man) this perfect soundness in the presence of you all." When Peter grabbed the lame man by the hand and commanded him to walk, the power of the Holy Spirit went into him and healed his body. The name of Jesus had more power than the sickness that was in the lame man.

In Ephesians 1:20-21, the Word says that Jesus is seated in heavenly places far above all principality and powers, and that His name is above every name. The name of Jesus has been given to the Body of Christ to use against anything that would have us bound. For approximately 25 percent of the people you pray for that need healing, you will have to take the name of Jesus and deal with the demon spirits that are behind the sickness before you can get them healed and set free. It's important that we read and meditate on the scriptures concerning the name of Jesus until we have faith in our hearts to cast out anything that kills, steals or destroys.

In Colossians 3:17 we are instructed to do everything in word and deed in the name of Jesus. If you can't say what you are saying in the name of Jesus, you shouldn't be saying it. Everything you do, and everywhere you go, you should do it in the name of Jesus. If you can't take Jesus with you, don't go.

Everything we bind or loose should be done with the name of Jesus. Always check on the spirit that is behind the sickness, and bind it with the name of Jesus and command it to leave and not return. Then take the name of Jesus and speak healing to the individual in the area of his or her need. Be bold in using the name of Jesus against the adversary. Accept nothing but total victory every time.

Steps for Using the Name of Jesus:
1. Read and meditate on the verses relating to the name of Jesus until you have faith in your heart in His name.
2. If it steals, kills or destroys you can use the name of Jesus and command it to leave.
3. Bind the spirit behind the sickness and command it to leave and not return until you are successful.
4. Resist any counterattack of sickness or bondage with the name of Jesus.
5. Do everything in the name of Jesus (Colossians 3:17).

Sample prayer: In the name of Jesus, I bind cancer (_____) and command it to leave this body and not return. I command sickness (_____) to leave and not return in Jesus' name. Fear (_____) I bind you in the name of Jesus and command you to leave and not return.

Chapter 5

Healing by Speaking to the Mountain

For verily I say unto you, That whosoever shall say unto this mountain (sickness), Be thou removed, and be thou cast into the sea; and shall not doubt in his heart, but shall believe that those things which he saith shall come to pass; he shall have whatsoever he saith.

Mark 11:23

Proverbs 18:21
Death and life are in the power of the tongue: and they that love it shall eat the fruit thereof.

Proverbs 12:18
There is that speaketh like the piercings of a sword: but the tongue of the wise is health (healing).

You can't believe one thing and confess something else and receive healing by faith from God for your physical body. Your believing and your confessing will have to line up with the Word of God and the things that you have petitioned God for, before the answer will manifest itself in the natural realm. If you study the four Gospels, you will never see Jesus confessing one thing and doing something else. He always followed His confession with His actions. Jesus and the Word of God are our example. Whatever Jesus did and the Word instructs us to do, that is what we are supposed to be doing each and every day of our lives. There is a spiritual law in the Bible that tells us we can never believe God above our confession (Proverbs 18:21).

The Bible informs us in Proverbs 18:21 that death and life are in the power of our tongue. We are speaking death or life to our surroundings with each word we speak. Every word that comes out of our mouth is edifying, positive, healing and victorious—or is encouraging death, sickness, defeat and bondage. In Mark 11:23 Jesus said, "That whosoever shall say unto this mountain (sickness), Be thou removed (leave my body), and be thou cast into the sea (don't come back); and shall not doubt in his heart (shall believe in his heart), but shall believe that those things which he saith (says) shall come to pass; he shall have whatsoever he saith (says)."

Sickness/disease is one of the mountains in our lives. We have to take the name of Jesus and rebuke the mountain (sickness) until it leaves. We need to speak to the mountain, calling it by name and commanding it to leave us and to not return in Jesus' name.

Make sure you understand this very important concept about speaking to the mountain of sickness. Just because you have made a negative confession or statement, it doesn't mean that it will come to pass within two days or at all. But if you *keep saying it*, sooner or later it will manifest itself in your life. In the Spirit realm, when we speak the Word of God, it is parallel to the natural realm, and it takes a period of time to bring the results into manifestation most of the time.

Proverbs 18:21 says that we have to love what we are saying before we can eat the fruit of it. If we have eaten the fruit of our mouth, this means that our confession has come to pass. If we have believed for healing for our body the fruit (healing) has already manifested itself. The Holy Spirit is responsible for confirming our confession as long as it agrees with God's Word. I would strongly recommend that if you have a sickness unto death, that you speak to the disease and command it to leave your body thousands of times each day.

In Mark 11:22-26 Jesus was giving us the principles of the Prayer of Faith or Petition. The Prayer of Faith or Petition is when you are requesting something from God. In verse 24 it tells us that, "What things soever ye desire when ye pray, believe that ye receive them, AND ye shall have them." What do you do between the time you pray the Prayer of Faith asking God for something and the manifestation of your answer? You put Mark 11:23 in the place of the "and" in Mark 11:24, and follow the instructions given to us in Mark 11:23. You speak to the sickness, telling it where to go and where to stay, until it leaves your body.

You can speak to the sickness as many times as you would like and still be in faith. Speak to the sickness and say, "sickness (cancer) I command you to leave my body and not return in the name of Jesus." Keep releasing faith on the mountain until you have what you want from God.

As we follow the instructions in these verses, we will speak to the mountain in line with the Word and in Jesus' name, telling it where to go and stay. We are to ask God to remove the sickness; however, we are never to ask God to speak to the mountain (sickness) for us. We are supposed to speak to the mountain ourselves.

It is not necessary for us to tell God, our heavenly Father, about the mountain, because He already knows about it. We speak to the mountain (sickness), but we pray to God in Jesus' name. The mistake most Christians make in prayer is that they want to pray to God and complain about their mountain (sickness). He told us to speak to the mountain (sickness) and to pray to Him.

When Abraham began to call those things that be not as though they were in Romans 4:17-21, he was strong in faith. His faith was strong because of his confession. **Your faith will only be as strong or as weak as your confession.** As long as you are speaking to the mountain, you are strong in faith. And if you will continue to speak to the sickness, it will eventually obey your confession and leave you.

We, as believers should not speak just anything we want to speak. Going around speaking words that are not supported by the Word of God, which consists of God's promises, is contrary to what God has instructed us to do. We always need to make sure when we are speaking to the mountain that we are speaking the Word of God. The Word (the promises of God) gives us the authority to speak to the mountain (sickness).

When we ask God for anything with our Prayer of Faith, we have to do the proper things in order to <u>receive</u> the answer. It is a lot easier to ask than to receive. Many Christians find it very difficult to stand on God's Word and receive the answer to their petition. The longer it takes to receive the answer, the harder it becomes, especially if we have pressure on us. That is one reason why we need to speak to the mountain (sickness) so many times each day, telling it to leave and not return.

The longer it takes to receive the answer, the bolder and louder you need to get! If the devil sees you getting weak with your confession, he knows he will outlast you. But, if you will stay strong, you will win every battle and receive your healing every time.

Another example of speaking to a mountain is when a sore throat attacks your body. Take the name of Jesus and speak to the sore throat and the cause of it, telling the soreness to leave your body and not return. Keep speaking to the mountain until it leaves your body. If you will begin to release faith by speaking to the mountain as soon as the attack begins on your throat, you can usually get rid of it in less than 30 minutes. The longer you put up with the sore throat, the longer it will take to get rid of it. Use this procedure against any sickness as soon as it attacks your body, and this will help you to walk in divine health.

We often set the stage or conditions that exist in our lives with our tongues. For instance, if someone is around me, including a family member, who has the flu, you will never hear me say I will get the flu. But what you will hear me say is, "I will never get the flu because I don't believe in having the flu."

This confession is a release of my faith, and I have not had the flu in over 25 years. I have actually slept with members of my immediate family who had the flu, but it could not jump over on me. The reason for this is that I had already released faith with my confession. Remember, death and life are in the power of our tongue. By taking an immediate stand against a sickness with your confession and faith, sometimes you can prevent the attack of sickness from even getting a foothold in your body.

The Bible never instructs us to ignore the devil. It does tell us to submit ourselves to God, and to resist the devil and he will flee from us (James 4:7). The main way you resist the devil and everything else that would rob you in life is with your tongue. You can't keep your mouth shut and resist the devil and his sickness. You will need to take a bold stand with your confession and drive the sickness from you.

You have to say "no" to sickness and disease. The best time to say no is before it attacks your body. Once you have been attacked with some kind of sickness, the Bible instructs you to speak to it, telling the sickness to leave you and not return. The longer you put up with the sickness in your body, the longer it will take to drive it out.

If you have a sickness unto death and you are confessing how sick you are and how bad you feel, you are not operating in faith. If the doctors can't help you, you will need to buy your casket because **you can't continually confess you are sick and believe God for your healing at the same time**. If you want God to heal you, you will have to release faith out of your mouth every hour of the day by commanding the sickness to leave your body and not return. While you are speaking to the mountain of sickness, make sure that you are believing that you are already healed based on God's Word (I Peter 2:24).

Sample Prayers

In the name of Jesus, I command _____ to leave my body and not return. I bind _____ and command it to leave my body. I receive healing in my body from the top of my head to the tip of my toes, and from the top of my head to the tip of my fingers in the name of Jesus.

I bind you sickness of _____, come out of my body. In the name of Jesus you have to leave me. By Jesus' stripes I am healed.

Mountain of _____, I am speaking to you. I bind you and command you to leave my body and not return. In the name of Jesus leave, now! Thank you, Jesus, for my complete healing.

Steps for Speaking to a Mountain (Sickness):
1. Always have chapter and verse for your confession so that you can speak according to God's will (I John 5:14).
2. Speak to the mountain consistently and out loud until it leaves. Tell it where to go and stay (Proverbs 18:21, Isaiah 55:11).
3. Speak healing into your body **in the name of Jesus** (I Peter 2:24, Matthew 8:17).
4. Get rid of all strife, worry, anxiety, and doubt (Philippians 4:4-8, Romans 10:17, I Peter 5:6-9).
5. Keep speaking, thanking, praising, and worshiping God until the answer manifests itself (Psalm 100).

Chapter 6

Healing Through Thanksgiving, Praise and Worship

Enter into his gates with thanksgiving and into his courts with praise: be thankful unto him, and bless his name.

Psalms 100:4

Colossians 4:2
Continue in prayer, and watch in the same with thanksgiving.

THANKSGIVING

Someone has said that all Bible-believing prayer should start off with thanksgiving and praise and end with thanksgiving and praise. If we really believe that God has heard and answered our prayer, you would think we would automatically thank Him for the answer. But it's the same in everything we do in life; if we want to follow instructions, it takes a conscious effort on our part.

Before Jesus raised Lazarus from the dead, He looked up to Heaven and said, "Father, I thank thee that thou hath heard me." All He did was thank His Father because He had already heard Him. This was because Jesus had already asked His Father to raise Lazarus from the dead and heal him before He got to the grave site. Then Jesus said, "Lazarus come forth." Lazarus then came forth alive and healthy (John 11:34-44).

If you look closely at what happened here you will find that Jesus didn't pray a long prayer. He only thanked God for hearing Him and then He spoke a command. Then Lazarus was raised from the dead and healed.

In Colossians 4:2 we are told to continue in prayer and watch with thanksgiving. After we pray and ask our heavenly Father for something in the name of Jesus, we should be thanking Him for the answer until we receive the manifestation. **As long as we are thanking God for the answer, we are in faith and the answer will always manifest itself.**

We can also receive our needs from God by just beginning to thank Him for the answer. We don't even need to pray about it if we don't want to. If we will keep thanking Him for our healing and not give up, the answer will always come.

Our thanksgiving has to be based on the promises of God. If we are in need of healing, we should know that God wants us healed because His Word informs us that healing belongs to the children of God.

Each day you should have a list of things that you are thanking God for. Sit down and write up a list of things that your heart desires. Make sure that divine healing and health are on the list.

As you spend time thanking God for those things on your list, you are releasing faith in these areas. After you have received the answer to one item on your list, erase it and add something else. Always keep divine health on your list of thanks. This is a great way of walking in faith in these areas.

Steps for Thanking God for Your Healing:
1. Decide what you are going to thank God for.
2. Have chapter and verse for your Thanksgiving.
3. Thank Him continually until you have your answer (I Thessalonians 5:18).

PRAISE

Psalm 150:1-6
1 Praise ye the Lord, Praise God in his sanctuary: praise him in the firmament of his power.
2 Praise him for his mighty acts: praise him according to his excellent greatness.

3 Praise him with the sound of the trumpet: praise him with the psaltery and harp.
4 Praise him with the timbrel and dance: praise him with stringed instruments and organs.
5 Praise him upon the loud cymbals: praise him upon the high sounding cymbals.
6 Let every thing that hath breath praise the Lord. Praise ye the Lord.

We are to offer "the sacrifice of praise to God continually, that is, the fruit of our lips giving thanks to his name" (Hebrews 13:15). Praising God is something we need to do each and every day. This will help to keep the line of communication open between the kingdom of Heaven and us. God will be able to bless us and meet every need we have if we keep ourselves open through thanksgiving, praise and worship.

We can praise God in the name of Jesus for anything. We can praise Him for healing, clothes, shoes, a home, a car, children, our job, our community, animals/pets, food, peace, joy, love, water, sleep, our government, leaders, pastors, teachers, our church, Heaven, salvation, Holy Spirit, guidance, protection, knowledge, wisdom, grace, victory, and anything else we can think of. We can praise Him in song in our native tongue, and we can praise Him in the Spirit (other tongues).

Most of what we call praise in the Church today is entertainment and emotionalism, and not really praise at all. Anything we do in the flesh is flesh and anything we do in the Spirit has to come out of our spirits. In the New Testament in Hebrews 13:15 we are told that praise should come out of our mouths. We should be praising from our hearts as it comes out of our mouths. Praising God is not based on our feelings; it should be based on the Word of God.

Believers today do a lot of things in church services that we call praise which actually have nothing to do with praise at all. Often the leader of the praise and worship service will ask the congregation to give the Lord a praise offering by clapping their hands. This is not praise, it is applause, and it is trying to bring God down to our level.

We need to go up to His level by praising Him with the fruit of our lips. We can praise God continually for His Word and His blessings. This will help us to keep the door to His blessings open, and then God can heal and deliver us.

In the Old Testament, people brought animals to the temple and sacrificed them to the Lord. Under the New Covenant, we come before His throne and praise Him, and this is our sacrifice before Him. Praising God for our healing will open our hearts so that we can receive healing for our minds and bodies. We can begin to praise God for the answer based on His Word, and never even pray about the problem--and have our needs met every single time.

We have a tendency in church services today to watch singers in front of the church singing to us, and the Church calls this praise. The singers might be praising God for themselves, but if we want the benefits of praising God, we will have to praise Him for ourselves. The praisers in the Body of Christ are the Christians in the congregation plus the music leaders. The praisers are not just the music leaders and the musicians on the platform--the praisers should include everybody in the congregation.

Always remember that I cannot praise God for you and you cannot praise God for me. We all have to praise God for ourselves. So open your mouth and praise God every day for your healing and victory in every area of your life.

Why Praise?
1. Praise helps you to receive the answer to your prayer. (Mark 11:24, Philippians 4:6)
2. Praise is your faith speaking. (Romans 4:20)
3. Praise is the strength of every believer. (Psalm 8:1-2)
4. Praise stops Satan in his tracks. (Psalm 8:2)
5. Praise delivers us from fear. (Psalm 34:1-4)
6. Praise makes your enemies fall and perish at God's presence. (Psalm 9:1-3)
7. Praise helps us not to be controlled by our emotions. (Hebrews 13:15)
8. Praise brings God on the scene personally. (Psalm 22:3)
9. Praise is a weapon. (II Chronicles 20:21-23)
10. Praise brings health. (Psalm 43:5)
11. Praise will free the prisoners. (Acts 16:25-26)
12. Praise is a perfect approach to God. (Psalm 100:1-5)
13. Praising God gives us favor with people. (Acts 2:47)

14. Praise helps us to control our thinking. (Philippians 4:8)
15. Praise in the Spirit (tongues) is praise beyond our intellect. (I Corinthians 14:17)

Steps for Praising God for Your Healing:
1. Have chapter and verse for your need.
2. Make a decision to praise God for the answer.
3. Cast down all thoughts that are contrary to what you are praising God for.
4. Keep praising God until you receive your answer.

WORSHIP

John 4:23-24
23 But the hour cometh, and now is, when the true worshippers shall worship the Father in spirit and in truth: for the Father seeketh such to worship him.
24 God is a Spirit: and they that worship him must worship him in spirit and in truth.

Jesus said in John 4:23-24 that he was making some changes in the area of worship. He said from this point on, they that worship God must worship Him in spirit and in truth. The word "truth" is easy to understand because it means worshiping in line with the Word of God, because God's Word is truth. When Jesus said that the true worshiper would have to worship God out of his spirit, these instructions changed the way the Church was to worship from that point of time until right now. If we are going to worship God, the worship has to come out of our spirits if it is to be true worship. We can't worship God from our heads if we are following the instructions that Jesus gave us.

Under the New Covenant, we can't read a songbook and worship God, because that would be singing out of our minds (soul realm) and not out of our spirits. If we were reading from an overhead screen, it would indicate that the words are coming out of our minds (soul). We could start off reading words in a worship song from a songbook or from an overhead screen, but they will not become true worship until they are coming out of our spirits. Most of the time after reading a chorus from a songbook or an overhead screen a few times, we can get it into our spirits and begin to worship God with it.

The Old Testament believers were not sons of God. They were servants of God because they were not born again. They were not born of the Spirit because the Holy Spirit had not recreated their spirits. Jesus had to shed His blood on the cross before anyone could get saved or born again. Because Jesus died for us, we can receive Him into our hearts and become born again by the Spirit of God.

Believers today are spiritually alive, whereas the Old Testament saints were spiritually dead. Everything they did as servants of God was done in the flesh. When they worshiped, it was a physical act rather then something that came out of their spirits. We can worship God out of our spirits because the Holy Spirit recreated our spirits, and He will help us worship God.

Jesus made another major change in worship in John 4:23-24. He said that the true worshiper would no longer worship in a certain place or in a special physical position. We can worship God anywhere and should especially do this in our prayer closet. Jesus said in the scripture above that we would worship in spirit. This means that our worship has to originate from our spirits. It has to flow out of us without our minds being in total control. Our minds have to be in agreement with what we are doing, but true worship can only come out of our spirits.

Jesus even gave us a word to use while worshiping. That word in John 4:23-24 is the word "worship." We can take the word "worship" and worship God our Father, and our Lord and Savior, the Lord Jesus Christ. We can worship God all day and night using this one word. In the sixth chapter of Isaiah, this prophet had a vision in which he saw the throne of God and the seraphims were around the throne worshiping God. They were using one word to worship God and that word was "holy." They were saying, "Holy, holy, holy, is the Lord of hosts: the whole earth is full of his glory" (Isaiah 6:3).

The Bible says that the posts of the door entering the throne room were moving and the throne of God was filled with glory. This was happening because the seraphims were worshiping God using one word and that was the word "holy." As far as we know, they are still worshiping today after thousands of years.

Again, today in many Christian churches, we sing many songs that we call worship that really are not worship at all. They might have a little praise in them, but many times all they are doing is helping us throw a pity party. We need to check on what we are singing and make sure that what we call worship is true worship. Sometimes it is difficult to find very many words to use while worshiping God. Some words you can use are adore, exalt, worship, glorify, honor, holy, bless, love, and magnify.

I believe that if the seraphims can worship God using one word and cause His glory to increase, we can use the word "worship" and bring an increase in His glory in our lives. If we will worship God out of our spirits, the glory of God will manifest itself out of us. We should never go into our prayer closet or attend a church meeting without worshiping God until His glory manifests itself in and through us. It only takes a few seconds of worship most of the time to start the glory flowing.

If we will worship God, He will heal our minds and bodies. He will heal our families, finances, jobs, businesses, homes, and everything else we have need of. Set aside time every day to worship God, and this will help keep you in a position where God can heal, deliver and set you free.

As we worship God, the glory of God will manifest itself in and around us. Jesus gave us His glory before He went back to Heaven in John 17:22 and I quote, "And the glory which thou gavest me I have given them (us); that they may be one, even as we are one." The glory of God is the presence of God. The atmosphere of heaven is glory, whereas the atmosphere of earth is air. When we get to heaven, we will not breathe air, but we will live in the glory of God!

When God's glory is increased in and around us, that is the atmosphere of Heaven in manifestation. Everything God has is in His glory. In His glory there is healing, deliverance, peace, strength, health, freedom, joy, prosperity, and everything we will ever have need of in this life. While we are worshiping God, the glory of God will increase in our lives (II Corinthians 4:18). We can go from glory, to glory, to glory while worshiping God. God's glory is enough to heal and deliver us in every area of our lives.

Steps for Worshiping God:
1. Have scriptures for worship (John 4:23-24).
2. Set aside time to worship God every day.
3. Worship God many times during the day and night.
4. Worship God for the things you are believing Him for.
5. Expect His glory to manifest itself in and around you as you worship. Make sure you release faith for your needs while the glory is in a strong manifestation.

Chapter 7

Healing Through the Prayer of Agreement

Again I say unto you, That if two of you shall agree on earth as touching any thing that they shall ask, it shall be done for them of my Father which is in heaven.

Matthew 18:19

Amos 3:3
Can two walk together, except they be agreed?

Jesus said in Matthew 18:19, "That if two of you shall agree on earth as touching any thing that they shall ask, it shall be done for them...." We can receive healing for our bodies through the Prayer of Agreement or we can minister to others by using this method. One of the first things we have to understand is that we have to be in agreement with God before any of this will work. The Bible says in Amos 3:3, "can two walk together except they be agreed?" We need to be in agreement with God, our Father, which means we always have to be in agreement with His Word. God's will for our life is His Word, and the Word is His will. Always try to have chapter and verse to back up your agreement.

Don't ever try to live the Christian life or follow God without following His Word. There are all kinds of false doctrines and cults in the world today, because people try to live a godly life without the Word of God. This is the same as trying to fly an airplane without having read the instruction booklet! You will have to know the handbook of instructions before you can fly the airplane, or you will probably crash before you can get off the ground. If you don't have God's Word for what you are agreeing upon, you will probably crash before you can get your prayer off the ground.

When you pray for someone else, the Prayer of Agreement is always in effect. The person you are praying for has to be in agreement with you. He or she has to agree with what you are saying before your prayer will work. There is a spiritual law found in the Word of God in Luke 12:48 which says, "...whomsoever much is given, of him shall be much required."

Whatever knowledge we have from the Bible or from the Kingdom of God, we are held accountable for it and have the responsibility in that area to walk it out. If we don't live and walk in line with what we know, God calls it "rebellion." He says rebellion is the same as witchcraft in I Samuel 15:23. Knowledge requires accountability in the

Kingdom of God, and we are held responsible for everything we have been taught.

Sometimes we think we can pray and force Christians to do things or force the things of God on them. But, if we pray for them and they don't agree with us, our prayers will not work. The easiest people to get healed are baby Christians because you can carry them on your faith. These are the individuals who don't know anything at all about the Word of God. They can agree with what you are saying very easily, and if they will agree with your Prayer of Agreement, it will work for them.

If the sick person doesn't know anything about divine healing, but will agree with your prayer, the responsibility to get them healed is on your shoulders. I always like to pray for the healing of a baby Christian because I know I can get them healed on my faith if they will agree with me.

If the Prayer of Agreement is being prayed and there are three people praying, all three cannot pray at the same time. If they did, all three of them could not totally agree on what is being said. One would have to pray and the other two agree, before all three could be in agreement with everything that was being prayed about. For example, if they were praying for someone who was sick and all three were praying at the same time, one could be praying for a successful operation, another could be praying for God to miraculously heal him, and another could be praying for the correct medication. There would be no agreement in this prayer and it would not work.

First, all three of them would have to decide what they wanted God to do. Then one person would have to pray while the other two agreed with him. Their prayer should always be based on chapter and verse from God's Word.

If you have 15 or more people praying for something, the same principle will apply. If you had 15 people praying for a certain thing and seven were in agreement and eight were not, the prayer would not be answered. It is harder to get a large number of people in agreement than a smaller number. Always decide on what you want to agree on before you pray. Then let one person pray and the others agree.

We often need someone to agree with us in the area of sickness at different times in our lives. Deuteronomy 32:30 says that two can do ten times more than one! The prayer of agreement can bring tremendous results in your life.

Anytime I have a lot of pressure on me in any area of my life, and the devil is trying to tell me I will not receive what I am believing God for, I always try to get someone involved in the Prayer of Agreement with me. I try to find someone who doesn't know what's going on in my life, so that the pressure that is on me will not influence him. That way, he can stay in agreement with my prayer and not waiver because of the circumstances in my life.

If you don't know anyone who can agree with you in the Prayer of Agreement, ask God to raise up someone so that you will have a prayer partner to agree with you. It is very important to have someone steadfast in faith that can agree with you on the subject of healing.

Five Steps to the Prayer of Agreement:
1. Have chapter and verse for your agreement.
2. Decide on what you want to agree on before you pray.
3. Only one person should pray and the others should agree.
4. Don't move off of your Prayer of Agreement until the answer has manifested itself.
5. Thank, praise and worship God until you have your answer.

Sample prayer: Father, we agree on the healing for _____. I command this sickness of _____ to come out of him and not return in the name of Jesus. I speak healing and health to every area of _____ body in the name of Jesus.

Chapter 8

Healing Through the Prayer of Binding and Loosing

Verily I say unto you, Whatsoever ye shall bind on earth shall be bound in heaven: and whatsoever ye shall loose on earth shall be loosed in heaven.

Matthew 18:18

Mark 3:27
No man can enter into a strong man's house, and spoil his goods, except he will first bind the strong man; and then he will spoil his house.

The main place where Jesus instructed us concerning the Prayer of Binding and Loosing is in Matthew 18:18 where He taught, "Whatsoever ye (you) shall bind on earth shall be bound in heaven: and whatsoever ye (you) shall loose on earth shall be loosed in heaven." We could say it this way, what we bind on Earth in the name of Jesus, Heaven will back us up, and what we loose on Earth, in the name of

Jesus, Heaven will back us up. The question you might have now is--what are we binding and loosing?

We can bind anything that kills, steals or destroys. When we bind the spirit of cancer in the name of Jesus and command it to leave an individual, it has to leave if everyone is in agreement. At the same time we cast out the cancer (disease), the individual is being loosed from the disease. In the areas of sickness and disease, you will notice that each illness has a name. The name of Jesus is above every name of any sickness or disease. So we take Jesus' name and bind the sickness and command it to leave the individual's body and not return.

The Bible tells us to resist the devil and he will flee from us (James 4:7). If we don't resist the sickness, it has a legal right to stay in our bodies. Under the New Testament, God will not automatically remove the sickness or demons from us. We have to resist them or someone else has to do it for us.

The Bible doesn't say in Matthew 18:18 that what God binds on Earth is bound in Heaven. What it does say is that what *you* and *I* bind on Earth is bound in Heaven. Our minds and bodies will automatically heal themselves if they can, but if they can't, we will have to bind the sickness or bondage and command it to leave in the name of Jesus.

We can bind the spirit of fear and command it to leave us in Jesus' name, and it will have to leave. This will free us from the bondage of the spirit of fear. Very often the prayer of binding and loosing works together. If someone had unforgiveness or bitterness in their heart, you could speak and loose the spirit of love (God's kind of love) into them, and if they will receive it, they would be loosed from their bondage. You can take the name of Jesus and command the person you are praying for to be loosed from all sickness, disease and bondage, and if they will receive your prayer, they will be set free.

It may be easier to understand the prayer of binding and loosing if we realize that there are three heavens that the Bible talks about. The third heaven is where God's throne is located. Paul said in II Corinthians 12:2, "I knew a man in Christ above fourteen years ago, (whether in the body, I cannot tell; or whether out of the body, I cannot tell: God knoweth;) such an one caught up to the third heaven." Most Bible scholars believe that Paul was talking about himself in this verse. God's throne is located above the stars, sun and moon. This is where the third heaven is located. The second heaven is located where the moon, sun and stars are located (Psalm 8:3).

The first heaven is described in Ephesians 6:12 which says, "For we wrestle not against flesh and blood, but against principalities, against powers, against the rulers of the darkness of this world, against spiritual wickedness in high places." This is the area where we live on Earth. It is the first heaven and this is the battleground where Christians are binding and loosing demon spirits to set the captives free.

Our binding and loosing is always done against the enemy of man, Satan, and his kingdom of darkness. Remember that the name of Jesus will bind sickness so that you can cast it out and loose the individual from all bondage.

When we are praying for a sick person, we should first find out what kind of sickness they have. The way we can find out this information is by asking them what is wrong, or by asking the Holy Spirit to reveal the sickness to us. Let's suppose it is a tumor. The name of Jesus is above the name "tumor."

Therefore, we need to bind the tumor in the name of Jesus, and command the tumor to die and come out of the body. We curse the seed and root of the tumor and command it to leave the body and to never return. Then we speak healing into the afflicted area and command the body to be healed, whole and healthy in the name of Jesus.

Most of the time when we bind something from the kingdom of darkness it is for the purpose of removing it from someone's life. When you bind any kind of sickness, always command it to leave and to not return in Jesus' name. If you are binding any kind of spirit of bondage make sure you command it to obey you and leave the person you are praying for.

There are evil spirits assigned over every country, city, town, family, and individual on earth (II Corinthians 4:4). Before any type of church service or Christian meeting begins, you should bind any spirit from interfering with the meeting and loose the Holy Spirit and angels to move in the meeting.

Before a bad spiritual atmosphere can be changed in a city, town, community, or any place, someone has to do some binding and loosing to stop the sin in that area. This will permit God to move and answer your prayers. If your city has a lot of murders going on in it, that murdering spirit will have to be bound before the murders will greatly decrease. It could be prostitution, drugs, stealing, or any other vice going on in the area. **The key to stopping anything that steals, kills or destroys is to bind the spirit that is behind it and loose the will of God in that area.**

You can bind the spirit of cancer, allergies, arthritis, asthma, bulimia, flu, deafness, diabetes, fear, gout, herpes, lupus, sclerosis, ulcers, and any other sickness and disease. Remember that everything we bind on earth, Heaven will automatically back us up. We do need the individual we are praying for to agree with us on what we are praying and believing God for. We can't override someone's will if they don't really want to be set free from sickness and disease.

The majority of the time when praying for the sick, you will need to do some binding and loosing in the name of Jesus. In order for us to remove the strong man (sickness), we should speak a bold command in line with the Word of God and in the name of Jesus. The bolder we are at times, the greater results we will have. The Holy Spirit will confirm what we are saying if it agrees with the Word of God.

Six Steps for Binding and Loosing:

1. Be bold when you use the name of Jesus against anything that steals, kills or destroys.
2. Identify the spirit with the Word of God, or ask the Holy Spirit to show you what spirit is causing the problem.
3. Bind the spirit (cancer, fear, bondage, lupus, etc.) and command it to leave and not come back.
4. If possible, spend time with the victim until he or she is free.
5. Give the person some scriptures to memorize and meditate on to take the place of bondage.
6. Instruct them to resist the spirit with the name of Jesus if it tries to come back on them.

Sample prayer: Cancer _____, I bind you in the name of Jesus and command you to come out of this person and not return. I curse the seed and root of this cancer and command it to die in the name of Jesus. I bind all the damage this disease has done in this body, and I command it to come out and the body to be totally healed. I bind the spirits of fear, bondage and death, and command them to come out in Jesus' name. I loose this person from all bondage by speaking God's love, joy, peace, strength, healing, and health in his or her mind and body in the name of Jesus.

Chapter 9

Healing Through Casting Out Demons

**Behold, I give unto you power to tread on
serpents and scorpions, and over all the power
of the enemy: and nothing shall by any means
hurt you.**

Luke 10:19

**Mark 16:17
And these signs shall follow them that believe;
In my name (Jesus) shall they cast out devils.**

**Acts 10:38
How God anointed Jesus of Nazareth with the
Holy Ghost and with power: who went about
doing good, and healing all that were oppressed
of the devil; for God was with him.**

Healing through casting demons out of people is an area
that most churches ignore. The reason for this is that most
Christians don't understand what the Bible has to say about
this subject. I firmly believe you will never be able to get

around 25 percent of sick people healed without knowing how to cast out demons. This was the approximate percentage Jesus ministered deliverance to out of all the sick people he prayed for in the Bible. You will often have to get the sick person delivered before you can get them totally healed.

We need to understand where these demons are located before we can comprehend how to deal with them. In I Thessalonians 5:23 the Word says we are a spirit (this is what is born again), we have a soul (mind, will, intellect, emotions), and we live in a body (earth suit). When we receive Jesus as our Lord and Savior, our spirits are born again, and we go from being a spiritually dead person to a spiritually alive one. Our spirits are recreated by the Holy Spirit and we become saved (Romans 10:9-10). We are born again (John 3:3-16). Our spirits are born again, but our minds and bodies are still the same as they were before we received Jesus Christ as our Lord and Savior.

We are responsible for doing something with our souls and bodies. Our soul (mind) has to be renewed with the Word of God (Romans 12:2). Our bodies have to be presented or given to God as an act of our will (Romans 12:1). We have to keep our minds renewed with the Word of God on a daily basis, and we need to keep our bodies under the control of the Word. This is something we need to practice each and every day.

We hear a lot of talk in the Body of Christ about whether or not a Christian can have a demon or be possessed by one. Let's define the meaning of these three words from Webster's dictionary: possession, oppression and depression. Possession means ownership or total control. Oppression means to be treated in a cruel or unjust manner, to feel burdened down or to experience a feeling of heaviness or suppression. Depression means an act of pressing down, sinking, lowering, sadness, gloominess, or low spirits. These are the three words that are used most often to indicate the presence of demons in someone in the Body of Christ. You need to understand that your spirit is the only thing that is born again, and a demon can't get into your spirit unless you have knowingly and willfully rejected your salvation, and most Christians would never do that. We are sealed with the Holy Spirit (Ephesians 1:13) until the day of redemption.

The problem lies in the area of our soul (mind) and body (earth suit). In James 4:7, the Bible instructs Christians to resist the devil and he will flee from them. Well, if we don't resist him, he will not leave. It is not automatic. We have to renew our minds with the Word of God, resist the devil, and then he will flee. Sometimes we see Christians that don't have their minds working right and the devil has them in bondage. You know, we can be sick in our minds as well as in our bodies. We need to keep our minds filled with God's Word and think, act and live in line with His Word.

Most believers in the Body of Christ have not renewed their minds with the Word of God on the subject of deliverance. That is why there is so much confusion, doubt and unbelief in this area. Ephesians 4:23 says, "And be renewed in the spirit of your mind." If our minds have not been renewed on the subject of deliverance, the devil can keep us confused and influence our lives in a negative way. Some churches even have their little children picking up demon spirits from TV programs, and they don't know what to do about it. There are psychics and fortunetellers on TV, and some churches even think this is from God!

We have all kinds of demonic activity going on around us, and most Christians don't even know that it is coming from the kingdom of Satan. We have to go to the Bible and find out what is from God and what is from Satan. This will only happen when our minds are renewed with the Word of God.

When ministering deliverance to anyone, try to get him or her in a position where you can spend some time with them. Identify the spirits that have them bound with the Word of God and by asking the Holy Spirit. Sometimes the person who is bound by the spirits can tell you their names. Demon spirits are proud of their names and they always name themselves after what they do.

Most people that need significant ministry will have more than one spirit that needs to be cast out of them. What the Bible calls the "strong man" in Mark 3:27 is the first demon spirit that enters into an individual. After the strong man enters someone, he will invite more demon spirits into the individual more wicked than himself. When casting out demons, always try to cast the strong man out first and the other demon spirits will then be easier to cast out.

Sometimes it takes time to get people delivered from demon spirits. Also, sometimes it takes time to get people healed. We cannot be successful until they have received total healing and deliverance. Time means nothing in the spirit realm. So if it takes five minutes or five hours, we should stay with the person needing help until he or she is free.

As long as we live on this earth, our bodies may sometimes be attacked with sickness and disease. For example, if a person has cancer they are not demon possessed, but a demon spirit is behind the disease, and we need to bind the spirit of cancer and cast it out. Then, they need to claim healing from all the damage the cancer has done to their body. At different times we might need to take the name of Jesus and cast out the spirit of fear (II Timothy 1:7) from our minds. Doing this at times will heal our minds and bodies.

God put us in charge of our minds and bodies, and we have to take care of them each and every day. Renewing our minds with the Word, and presenting our bodies to God our Father as a living (not dead) sacrifice, will keep us free from all bondage.

In Acts 10:38 we see that everyone Jesus healed was oppressed by the devil. We know that Jesus cast demons out of around 25 percent of all the people He prayed for during His three and one-half year ministry. In I John 3:8 it informs us that Jesus came to destroy the works of the devil.

When Jesus left the earth, He gave us authority in His name to cast out devils and to heal the sick. In Luke 10:19 Jesus said, "I give unto you (your name) power to tread on serpents and scorpions, and over all the power of the enemy (devil): and nothing shall by any means hurt you." The Body of Christ has the power and authority over all demon spirits. We should be controlling them--they should not be controlling us.

There are many spirits mentioned in the Bible such as rebellion, infirmity, alcohol, drugs, lying, envy, witchcraft, deceit, anger, ego, perversion, cults, homosexuality, adultery, incest, rape, black magic, strife, bondage, pride, gluttony, worry, depression, jealousy, grief, fear, dumb, deaf, seducing, and sorrow--and these are only a few of them. We should take the name of Jesus and control any and all demon spirits that try to influence our lives. We can control and reject everything that Satan tries to put on us with the name of Jesus and the power of the Holy Spirit.

We will need an agreement from those we are praying for before we can control and remove most demon spirits from them. Command the demon spirits to come out of those you are praying for until they leave. Sometimes it will take hours to get someone delivered and set free from demon spirits. Other times, it will take only minutes to get them set free. Don't get in a hurry when ministering deliverance, because the devil will try to wear you out and cause you to give up before the person is totally delivered. Take your time and enjoy what you are doing for your heavenly Father!

Steps For Casting out Demons:
1. Pray, fast, read and meditate on the Word so you will be ready to cast out demons.
2. Use the name of Jesus and be bold until you have results. Remember, time means nothing in the spirit world.
3. Ask the Holy Spirit to guide and lead you as you minister deliverance.
4. Thank, praise and worship your heavenly Father in Jesus' name. Make sure you are enjoying yourself and having a good time while you are working in the realm of deliverance.

Sample prayer: Spirit of fear, I bind you in the name of Jesus and command you to come out and not return. I speak the peace of Jesus into this individual's mind and body. Thank you, Jesus, for setting them free.

Chapter 10

Healing Through Calling for the Elders of the Church and Anointing with Oil

Is any sick among you? Let him call for the elders of the church; and let them pray over him, anointing him with oil in the name of the Lord.

And the prayer of faith shall save the sick, and the Lord shall raise him up; and if he have committed sins, they shall be forgiven him.

James 5:14-15

Mark 11:23-24

For verily I say unto you, That whosoever shall say unto this mountain, Be thou removed, and be thou cast into the sea; and shall not doubt in his heart, but shall believe that those things which he saith shall come to pass; he shall have whatsoever he saith.

Therefore I say unto you, What things soever ye desire, when ye pray, believe that ye receive them, and ye shall have them.

Another way we can receive our healing is by calling for the elders of the church to anoint us with oil. Then they will pray the Prayer of Faith over us, and God will heal us and raise us up from our sickbed.

There are a few instructions in these verses that we need to follow. If we don't follow these instructions, we will not receive our healing in this manner. The first thing the sick person is supposed to do is to call for the elders of the church. The word "elder" here doesn't mean an old man of 60 years. He could be 60 years old and not even believe in divine healing!

As long as the elder believes in divine healing and knows how to pray the Prayer of Faith for the sick, he or she qualifies for the job. God is no respecter of persons (Romans 2:11). He will use anyone who is willing to let Him anoint them and He will heal the sick through them. God will even use small children to pray for the sick.

But notice in James 5:14 that the sick person has to call for the elders--it can't just be someone else calling the elders for the sick person. If the sick person will call the elders for prayer, then the stage is set for him or her to receive their healing.

The second thing that must take place is that the elders need to anoint the sick person with oil in the name of Jesus. Oil represents the Holy Spirit, and the Holy Spirit is our healer (Romans 8:11). You don't have to pour a gallon of oil on the sick person, all you need to do is wet your finger with the oil and touch their forehead. But, if the Holy Spirit leads you to use more oil, feel free to do so.

The third thing that should take place is that the elders should pray the Prayer of Faith for the sick person. There are two other places where the Prayer of Faith is located in the New Testament and they are in Mark 11:22-26 and Matthew 21:22. I want to emphasize that the elders need to believe in and know how to pray the Prayer of Faith. They need to believe that the sick are healed by faith when they pray for them. A lot of elders in many churches don't even believe in divine healing or that God will heal people today. Make sure you don't call unbelieving elders if you need someone to pray for your healing. If you don't know any elders that will pray for you, pray and ask God to send someone to you that will pray for you, and then believe Him for your healing.

When we pray the Prayer of Faith for someone, we should be basing our prayer on the Word of God. The Bible tells us that by Jesus' stripes we were healed in I Peter 2:24. This scripture informs us that healing is past tense in the mind of God. He healed us 2,000 years ago when Jesus bore our sickness at the time those stripes were put on His back. We should proclaim this by faith as we pray for the sick.

In Hebrews 11:1 the Word informs us that faith is the substance (proof) of things hoped for and the evidence of things not seen. We believe by faith that the sick are healed when we pray for them. The only evidence we have until the healing manifests itself is our faith, which is in the Word of God. Mark 11:24 tells us to believe that we have received the answer to our prayer when we pray, and then we shall have it. The believing comes first, and the receiving comes second.

After the Prayer of Faith has been prayed, the Lord will raise up the sick person and heal him. The last part of the verse in James 5:15 says, "if he have committed sins, they shall be forgiven him." This applies to Christians and unbelievers. Normally, however, if we have sinned, we need to ask God to forgive us in the name of Jesus and He said He would. If the sick person is a nonbeliever, we should ask him to pray the sinner's prayer and get born again.

Steps for Calling the Elders and Anointing with Oil:
1. The sick person should call for the elders of the church that believe in James 5:14-15.
2. The elders should anoint with oil in the name of Jesus.
3. The elders should pray the Prayer of Faith.
4. The Lord forgives and raises up the sick person and heals him.
5. Give the sick person some scriptures and show him how to use them to keep his healing.
6. Thank, praise and worship God for the healing.

Sample prayer: Father, I anoint this person with oil in the name of Jesus. I ask you to heal him/her of _____, and I thank you that they are healed in the name of Jesus. Father, I thank you for healing this person in Jesus' name.

Chapter 11

Healing Through the Prayer of Commitment

> **Therefore take no thought (anxious thought), saying, What shall we eat? or, What shall we drink? or, Wherewithal shall we be clothed? (For after all these things do the Gentiles seek:) for your heavenly Father knoweth that ye have need of all these things.**
>
> **But seek ye first the kingdom of God, and his righteousness; and all these things shall be added unto you.**
>
> **Take therefore no thought (anxious thought) for the morrow: for the morrow shall take thought for the things of itself. Sufficient unto the day is the evil thereof.**
>
> **Matthew 6:31-34**

There are times in our lives when we can't receive healing for our minds or bodies because we are worried, anxious, fearful, uptight, or fretting over something. Until we do something about these things that have pressure on us and that are keeping us in bondage, we can't open our hearts to God our Father and receive healing from Him.

Sometimes we will need to pray the Prayer of Commitment, which involves rolling all of our cares, worries and anxieties over on Jesus before we can be healed.

There is no fear, worry or anxiety in God's kingdom. Most fear and worry come from Satan and the kingdom of darkness (II Timothy 1:7). When you are filled with fear, worry and the cares of this world, your body chemistry gets off balance. Your glands and organs are overactive or under-active. This causes your metabolism to be off, and it will bring all kinds of sickness and disease on you.

When you pray for someone who is living under these conditions, or if you are praying and believing for yourself to be healed, healing will not last if fear, worry, cares and their effects on your body and mind exist. The individual needing healing will have to change their attitude and get free from all bondage (worry, fear and anxiety) before their healing can be a permanent thing.

The Bible tells us in Proverbs 3:5 to trust in the Lord with all your heart and lean not unto your own understanding. If we are trusting in the Lord Jesus, we can't be worried and uptight about what is going on around us. When we trust our heavenly Father we will be free, especially on the inside.

Being free from worry, anxiety and fear sounds good, but how do we actually accomplish this? Jesus told us in Matthew chapter six not to even worry about the food we eat each day and to take no thought (worrying thought) for tomorrow. If Jesus told us not to worry, we can follow His instructions that He gave us throughout the Bible in this area.

If we neglect to follow His instructions, we will almost without a doubt be in bondage because there are so many things coming at us from the world, the flesh, and the devil that we will be tormented all the time. We have TV, newspapers, magazines, families, jobs, finances, doctors, bodies, sicknesses, and many other things coming at us to apply pressure to our lives each day. The devil uses all of these things to try to get us to worry ourselves half to death! Jesus told us not to worry, and that means we can live a life free from worry. Hallelujah!

In II Corinthians 10:4-5 the Word gives us three steps Satan uses to bring us into mental and emotional bondage and to control our lives. These three things are thoughts, imaginations and strongholds. Let's take a closer look at these three steps so we can understand how the devil can trick us and bring us into bondage, and even more importantly how we can avoid falling into his trap.

A thought is the first thing that we will pick up in our minds when something negative happens around us. If we let this thought stay in our mind, and if we keep running it over and over through our mind for a period of time, it becomes an imagination. Here, we analyze and think about the thought over and over and over. The more we think about it, the more we worry about it. The more we worry about it, the more our minds and bodies get anxious and uptight. We do need to analyze different things going on in our lives at times, but once we have evaluated them, we need to make a decision about the problem and quit thinking about it over and over.

The thought will then automatically become an imagination if we expound and dwell on it over a long period of time. Now we are at the point where we are running the thought through our mind day and night. Sometimes we will catch ourselves even waking up from sleep at night worrying about the problem. Now the problem has become a stronghold in our lives.

A stronghold is something that has a certain amount of control over you. We need to get rid of the stronghold or it will bring depression and sickness on us every time. Many people have died young because of the strongholds and related bondages in their lives. We have to get rid of the thoughts that cause the imaginations by taking the name of Jesus and commanding the stronghold to leave and not return.

Remember, Jesus said that we *could* live a life of freedom—and freedom from mental torment means to be carefree, worry-free, burden-free and anxiety-free. When any negative thoughts try to come into your mind, cast them out in the name of Jesus. Don't let the devil use your mind for a garbage dump. Keep it free from worry and filled with the Word of God. As you do this, your body will stay chemically balanced and heal itself. This will enable you to walk in victory each and every day of your life.

Luke 21:34-36
34 And take heed to yourselves, lest at any time your hearts be overcharged with surfeiting, and drunkenness, and cares of this life, and so that day come upon you unawares.
35 For as a snare shall it come on all them that dwell on the face of the whole earth.
36 Watch ye therefore, and pray always.
I Peter 5:6-9
6 Humble yourselves therefore under the mighty hand of God, that he may exalt you in due time:
7 Casting all your care upon him; for he careth for you.
8 Be sober, be vigilant; because your adversary the devil, as a roaring lion, walketh about, seeking whom he may devour:
9 Whom resist stedfast in the faith....

Jesus told us in Luke 21:34-36 that one of the signs of the end times is that some Christians would have their hearts overcharged with drunkenness and the cares of this life. When I first read these verses, I thought that the word drunkenness was referring to drinking too much alcohol, but that is not what these verses are talking about. In I Peter 5:6-9 one of the things we are instructed to do is to be sober. These verses are talking about being drunk on the cares and worries of this world.

Have you ever been so worried about something that you could not make a quality decision about what you were worrying about even if your life depended on it? Sure you have! Have you ever been so worried about something that you couldn't eat and your stomach was hurting? Maybe you were so worried that you couldn't even sleep at night. Christians are having nervous breakdowns because they are worrying too much—this should not be happening!

And unfortunately, most of the time what we are worried about is actually not that important. Many times our worries are needless, and the situations that we fear may happen never even occur. Sometimes believers end up worrying themselves to death over the things going on around them. This is actually what the Bible calls being drunk on the worries and cares of life. Jesus said to be sober by rolling all your cares and worries over on Him.

If a Christian got drunk on alcohol we would realize he had a problem that needed to be corrected. But if the same Christian got drunk on the cares and worries of life, we would ignore him and act like nothing was wrong. When Christians get drunk on the cares and worries of life, they need healing and deliverance.

Philippians 4:4-8
4 Rejoice in the Lord always: and again I say, Rejoice.
5 Let your moderation be known unto all men. The Lord is at hand.

6 Be careful for nothing; but in every thing by prayer and supplication with thanksgiving let your requests be made known unto God.
7 And the peace of God, which passeth all understanding, shall keep your hearts and minds through Christ Jesus.
8 Finally, brethren, whatsoever things are true, whatsoever things are honest, whatsoever things are just, whatsoever things are pure, whatsoever things are lovely, whatsoever things are of good report; if there be any virtue, and if there be any praise, think on these things.

In these verses in Philippians 4:4-8 we are instructed to "be careful for nothing" or we could say it this way, "do not worry or be anxious for anything." If we want the peace of God in our hearts, we have to learn how not to worry or be anxious over *anything*. In verse eight we are also told how to think at all times. We are instructed to only think on whatsoever things are true, honest, just, pure, lovely, and of a good report.

These are the things we should be thinking on. And some virtue and praise has to be in something before we are allowed to think on it for any length of time! It can be honest but if it's not a good report, then we are not supposed to think on it. If it is true but not lovely, then we are not supposed to think on it either. It has to line up with all six directives and then have some virtue and praise in it before we are allowed to think on it for any length of time.

God wants us free to think and meditate on His Word, and not be in bondage to the devil. Keep your thoughts positive and free from bondage, and the peace of God will reside in your heart and mind.

How to Live Above the Pressures of the World, the Devil, and Circumstances:

1. Find out what the Word of God and the Holy Spirit say about any problem you are facing.
2. Analyze and evaluate the problem or condition.
3. Make a decision as to what you want to do about the problem.
4. Then roll all the cares, worries, fears, anxieties, and all negative thoughts over on Jesus. Give Him the whole load. Dump it all on Jesus and don't take it back.
5. Thank, praise and worship while your heavenly Father works on the problem, and until you receive your answer.

Sample prayer: Father, I roll all my worries and anxieties over on Jesus. I give Him all my problems and I receive His love, joy and peace in my mind and body. I am going to live carefree, worry-free, burden-free, and anxiety-free in the name of Jesus. Thank you, Jesus, for setting me free!

Chapter 12

Healing Through Prayer Cloths

And God wrought special miracles by the hands of Paul:
So that from his body were brought unto the sick handkerchiefs or aprons, and the diseases departed from them, and the evil spirits went out of them.

Acts 19:11-12

Matthew 14:36
And besought him (Jesus) that they might only touch the hem of his (Jesus') garment: and as many as touched were made perfectly whole.

Romans 2:11
For there is no respect of persons with God.

We see in the four Gospels that when someone touched Jesus in faith, power would go out of Him and heal them. In Mark 5:25-34 we see the woman with the issue of blood come up behind Jesus and touch His garment. She had been sick for twelve years, and had spent all her money on doctors, but she was getting worse rather than getting better. When she touched Jesus' garment, the power of the Holy Spirit came out of Him, went into the woman's body, and healed her.

In Matthew 14:35-36 the men of Gennesaret went out in all the country and brought all the sick and diseased to Jesus. They asked Him if they could touch the hem of His garment, and everyone that touched Jesus' garment was healed. There were probably thousands of people in the crowd that touched Jesus that day, and the healing power went out of Him through His clothes and healed them.

You might ask the question, "what does this have to do with me? I need to be healed and Jesus is not walking on the earth today like He was 2,000 years ago. He's in heaven now." You are absolutely correct! Jesus is in heaven seated at the right hand of God, our Father. But Jesus gave all authority to the Church (born again believers), and He told us to go forth and heal the sick (Mark 16:15-18, Matthew 28:18-20).

We have the same Holy Spirit that Jesus had, and Jesus gave us His name to take the place of Him being on earth physically. His name is above the name of every sickness on earth. When we anoint a prayer cloth, it is always done in the name of Jesus. Remember, in Hebrews 13:8 it tells us that, "Jesus Christ is the same yesterday, and to-day and for ever." Whatever Jesus did in Matthew, Mark, Luke, and John, He will do today. However, today He does it through

His Church (the Body of Christ), which consists of those who are born again and washed in His blood.

We have an example in Acts 19:11-12 where Paul laid his hands on handkerchiefs and aprons and sent them out to sick people. When anointed cloths were laid on the people, the diseases departed from them and evil spirits left them. The handkerchiefs and aprons transported the anointing and power of the Holy Spirit from Paul's body to the sick. When they were laid on the sick, the anointing went into their bodies and healed their diseases and drove the demons out of them.

Most evangelistic ministries will anoint a prayer cloth and mail it to you if you will ask them. When I anoint a prayer cloth, I pray just like I would pray if the sick person were right there with me. I bind sickness, bondage and demons, and command them to leave the person's mind and body in the name of Jesus. I speak healing, health and deliverance into the individual. When I get finished praying and laying my hands on the cloth, I know it is anointed to heal and deliver the sick. Through the use of a prayer cloth, the anointing we have in us can be transferred from our hands to someone that is sick or in bondage by using the name of Jesus. We know this is true because the Word of God gives us the example in Acts 19:11-12.

One of the most unusual miracles I have ever experienced with prayer cloths happened at a Full Gospel Business Men's meeting one night in 1980. I was the president of the chapter and we had a very anointed speaker in the area of healing that night. After he had spoken and we had prayed for everyone in the meeting, we began to pray for the officers in the chapter.

At the end of the meeting our music leader said he had a friend in the hospital dying of cancer, whom the doctors said would be dead in less than three days. Our music leader was looking around for a handkerchief and couldn't find one. So he went into the bathroom and got a paper towel. We anointed the paper towel with some oil that we found in the restaurant and laid hands on it and prayed for the man's healing. The next day our music leader took the paper towel to the hospital and told the gentleman what we had done. He then pinned the paper towel on him. Three days later, he was released from the hospital and went home completely healed!

If we can't go to where the sick are located, anointing and praying over handkerchiefs and cloths is a very important method we can use to get them healed. We should have prayer cloths traveling around the world carrying the anointing of the Holy Spirit to heal the sick. If you have never used this method in your personal life to pray for the sick, I would like to encourage you to start implementing it as soon as possible. Be bold, do what God wants you to do, and He will take care of the healing!

Steps for Praying over Prayer Cloths:
1. Lay hands on the prayer cloth and pray for what you want to happen. Pray the Prayer of Faith and any other prayer you want to pray.

2. Send the prayer cloth to the individual who needs healing and deliverance, and tell them what was done and encourage them to believe God for their healing.

3. Release faith in the name of Jesus, thanking Him because it is done.

4. Stay in agreement with what was done by faith, and don't let the devil talk you out of it.

5. Thank, praise and worship God until the healing is complete.

Chapter 13

Healing Through Intercessory Prayer

I exhort therefore, that, first of all, supplications, prayers, intercessions, and giving of thanks, be made for all men.
For kings, and for all that are in authority: that we may lead a quiet and peaceable life in all godliness and honesty.

I Timothy 2:1-2

Galatians 4:19
My little children, of whom I travail (intercede) in birth again until Christ be formed in you.

What is intercessory prayer? It's a prayer for others. An intercessor is one who takes the place of another and pleads their case. This is another way we can receive our healing-- that is having someone who will intercede for us until we are healed. This type of praying can be done in your native tongue or in other tongues, which is praying in the Holy Ghost.

I have seen many sick people healed through intercessory prayer, but it will not work 100 percent of the time. The reason why it will not work 100 percent of the time is that you can't always override the sick person's will. In fact, sometimes it is easier to get a sinner healed using intercessory prayer than an older Christian. But, if you can get the sick person to agree with you, your intercessory prayer will work every time.

Let's take a look at why God needs an intercessor. This will help us understand why we need to intercede and pray for the world and everything in it, including sickness and disease. When God created Adam and Eve, He put them in the Garden of Eden. He gave Adam authority over all the earth and everything on it. He told them not to eat of the fruit of the tree of the knowledge of good and evil. He went on to say that if they did eat of that fruit they would surely die.

God made man and gave him a free will. Man was not programmed like an animal because he could make any decision he chose to make, even if it was wrong. Adam and Eve ate the fruit from the tree of the knowledge of good and evil and died spiritually, but not physically. Satan then became the god of this world's system, because Adam gave it to him by disobeying God and obeying Satan. Spiritual death not only entered into Adam and Eve when they sinned, but was passed on to every human being born into this earth since then. Because of Adam's sin the devil began to dominate the human race. Jesus then came to earth and died on the cross for man's sins thereby paving the way for man's redemption and acceptance into the Kingdom of God.

But there was one thing that man never lost and that was his ability to make decisions. Even today, God is limited in moving on this earth until someone asks Him to do something. Man can ask God to do something, and He will do it just because man asked Him. But we should always ask for things according to God's Word.

In Genesis chapters 18 and 19 we find Abraham interceding for Sodom and Gomorrah because of their sins. Abraham asked God if He would destroy the cities if there were 50 righteous people found there and God said no. Well, there were not 50 righteous found in Sodom and Gomorrah. So Abraham kept interceding for those two cities until he got God down to ten righteous people. Abraham asked God if ten righteous people were found in Sodom and Gomorrah would He destroy them, and God said He wouldn't destroy them.

Perhaps, Abraham should not have stopped at ten, he should have kept on going until he got to five or less. But he stopped at ten people and since there were not ten righteous people in the two cities, God destroyed Sodom and Gomorrah. This is an example of how important intercessory prayer is in our lives. We can change our lives, surroundings, and even our cities with intercessory prayer! We can also get the sick healed through intercessory prayer.

Ezekiel 22:30 describes how God was looking for an intercessor to stand in the gap for the land. Today more than ever, God is looking for intercessors to stand in the gap and pray for those who are sick, bound and tormented by the devil. Remember, sickness and disease steals, kills and destroys according to John 10:10, and it comes from the kingdom of darkness, Satan and his demons. We have to take a stand and intercede against sickness, so God can set us free.

The Bible informs us in Hebrews 7:25 and Romans 8:34 that Jesus is seated at the right hand of God, our Father, in heaven making intercession for us. He intercedes for us continually. Romans 8:22-28 informs us that the Holy Spirit is on earth making intercession for us. The Holy Spirit will intercede through us in other tongues as we pray for the sick. Also, He will help us pray in our native tongue.

We have Jesus in heaven interceding for us, and we have the Holy Spirit on earth interceding for us. With Jesus and the Holy Spirit interceding for Christians, we should never lose a battle to sickness. We, as Christians, are supposed to be interceding for one another all the time. There should be intercessory prayer going forth all the time for the Body of Christ and for the things of the world.

We can intercede and pray in English, or in our native tongue for someone's healing. Our prayer should be based on chapter and verse from the Bible. We should pray the Prayer of Faith and other types of prayers, believing the person was healed when we prayed. We should use the name of Jesus and bind and loose so that all the person's needs are met. Then, we can thank, praise and worship God until he or she is healed.

You can also intercede and pray in the Spirit, with other tongues, until the sick person receives their healing. Sometimes while praying in other tongues you may even experience some symptoms that the sick person has in their body. Don't let this bother you! Just keep praying until the symptoms leave your body and you have a note of victory. Sometimes, when the symptoms leave your body, they also leave the person you were interceding for. This doesn't happen all the time, only on rare occasions.

Sometimes you need to intercede for the sick until you have victory on the inside. The victory comes when you sing, laugh, or God's peace and joy manifest in your spirit. Spend as much time interceding for the sick person by praying in other tongues as your time will allow. The more you pray, the faster they will receive their healing most of the time.

Steps for Interceding for the Sick:
1. Have chapter and verse to back up your intercession.
2. Make a decision as to what you're believing God for in intercession. Be bold and keep interceding until you have the answer.
3. Intercede in your native tongue and in other tongues.
4. Always do plenty of thanking, praising and worshiping God.

Chapter 14

Healing Through the Laying On of Hands

> And these signs shall follow them that believe;
> In my name....
> They shall lay hands on the sick, and they shall
> recover.
>
> **Mark 16:17-18**

Hebrews 6:1-2
**Therefore leaving the principles of the doctrine
of Christ, let us go on unto perfection; not
laying again the foundation of repentance from
dead works, and of faith toward God,
Of the doctrine of baptisms, and of laying on of
hands, and of resurrection of the dead, and of
eternal judgment.**

The laying on of hands is a doctrine of the Church. God,
in Hebrews 6:1-2, informs all believers that they should
have been taught this fundamental doctrine concerning the
laying on of hands from the leaders of the Church. The
problem with the Church is that most Christians have never

been taught what the Bible says about this subject. Therefore, they don't know how to move in this fundamental doctrine. In Mark 16:15-18 Jesus said that all Christians (believers) should lay hands on the sick in His name and that they would recover. If we really believe what Jesus is saying in these scriptures, all believers would be more than happy to lay hands on the sick in His name and see God heal them.

When we lay hands on someone in the name of Jesus, we release the power and anointing of the Holy Spirit that we have on the inside of us to flow into the sick person. If they will receive the anointing of the Holy Spirit, it will heal their mind and body. As a Christian, whatever is on the inside of you can be released through your hands. There are people who delve into the occult and they release and send demon spirits into people with their hands. Everything the devil does is a counterfeit, so all he is doing is imitating God. God put His power and anointing into His children's hands so they can help other people who have need of healing and deliverance.

Jesus told us in John 14:12 that we would do the works that He did and that we would do even greater works! Jesus laid His hands on the deaf, the dumb, the blind, lepers, and people with all types of sicknesses and diseases. He laid His hands on Peter's mother-in-law and healed her of a great fever. Jesus laid His hands on Jairus' daughter and raised her from the dead. He laid His hands on little children and blessed them. He laid His hands on the woman who had a spirit of infirmity for 18 years and cast the spirit out and healed her. Jesus healed the multitudes by laying His hands on them.

If we study the early Church, we see that this was also a common practice among them as well. Acts 28:8 describes how Paul laid his hands on Publius' father and healed him. In Acts 19:11-12 Paul did special miracles by laying his hands on aprons and handkerchiefs, and as they touched the bodies of sick people, they were healed. In Iconium Paul and Barnabas did many signs and wonders with their hands (Acts 14:3).

Scripture goes on to tell us that by the hands of the apostles many signs and wonders were done (Acts 5:12). Ananias, a lay person, laid hands on Paul and he was healed and filled with the Holy Spirit in Acts 9:17. Peter and John laid hands on the Samaritans and they received the Holy Spirit. In Numbers 27:18-23 God told Moses to lay hands on Joshua and transfer the power and authority to him. We can see people in the Old Testament and New Testament who laid hands on different individuals and transferred the power, glory and anointing of the Holy Spirit to others. We have the same Holy Spirit in us, and we can transfer the Holy Spirit's healing power to the sick through our hands.

Most born again Christians, who have been practicing this doctrine in the Church over the years, are those that are Spirit-filled with the evidence of speaking with other tongues. In my own life, I was 38 years old before I ever laid hands on a sick person and prayed for one. I didn't have the boldness or the knowledge to lay hands on anyone that was sick until I received the baptism of the Holy Spirit with the evidence of speaking in other tongues (Luke 11:11-13, Acts 2:4). Once I realized that the power of the Holy Spirit, which was in me, could be transferred to a sick person and get them healed, I began to exercise faith in this area and lay hands on the sick whenever I had the opportunity.

If you would like to be filled with the Spirit, read the scriptures on receiving the fullness of the Spirit. Then, ask God to fill you with the Holy Spirit, and this will give you the boldness to lay hands on the sick and to pray for them. There is also a prayer in the back of this book to receive the fullness of the Holy Spirit.

Sometimes we need to lay hands on ourselves and release the power of the Holy Spirit along with our faith when we need healing. If we will do this, it will release the power of the Holy Spirit and the glory of God in the area in which we need healing so we can be set free.

There are different ways to administer the laying on of hands. I have been in small prayer groups where the leaders would sit someone down in a chair and everyone would lay their hands on him or her and pray for their healing. Sometimes the sick person would just stand and we would lay hands on them and pray.

In some church services, people stand around the altar while church leaders lay their hands on them and pray for their healing. I have even been in church services or large meetings in convention centers where an evangelist would ask the congregation to lay hands on each other and pray for one another. Under these conditions, make sure you know who is laying hands on you. You always have to remember that whatever spirit they have on the inside of them can be transferred to you.

There is one area regarding the laying on of hands in which the Church has had a lot of teaching on over the last 20 years. This is in the area of spinal problems. Charles and Frances Hunter have really developed these teachings over the years. They have books and videotapes on these subjects, and I would highly recommend them to you if you have a back problem, or if you would like to learn how to pray for people with such problems.

The Hunters have given specific names to various commands to adjust the spine and heal the back. These names are "growing out legs and arms," "the pelvic thing" and "the neck thing." I have heard Charles and Frances Hunter, Dr Roy LeRoy, a chiropractor, and many others say, that around 60 to 80 percent of all sickness can be traced back to the spinal cord and the nerves of the body. They say that if you can get the spine and nerves healed and adjusted, the body will automatically heal itself.

When "growing out arms," have the person stand up straight, put their feet together so that their toes are even, and they're looking forward. Have them extend their arms in front of them with the palms of their hands facing each other, about one-half inch apart, and have them stretch their arms out straight as far as they can. Check their arms to see if one is shorter than the other. If they have a short arm, grow it out by commanding their spine, muscles, tendons, ligaments, and nerves to be adjusted and to rotate into proper position. Also, command the shoulders to be level.

Always make such commands in the name of Jesus and by the power of the Holy Spirit. Command the discs and vertebrae to be healed and to go into proper position. Command the short arm to grow out even with the other one, and command everything to be healed in the name of Jesus.

To pray for lower back problems, have the person sit all the way back in a chair. Pick their feet up and check the length of their legs to see if one leg is shorter than the other. Command their sacrum area to be adjusted and all the vertebrae and discs to be healed and to rotate into proper position and to stay there. Command the spirit of arthritis to leave and not return in the name of Jesus. Command the muscles, ligaments, tendons, and nerves to adjust and go into place, and the short leg to grow out even with the other one in the name of Jesus. Speak healing from God's Word to any and all problems in their back in the name of Jesus.

When doing "the neck thing," face the person you are praying for and put your hands on each side of their face and neck. Wrap your fingers around their neck until they touch over the spinal column. Command all muscles, ligaments, tendons, vertebrae, discs, and nerves to rotate into proper position and be healed in the name of Jesus. Speak any other command that the Holy Spirit leads you to say.

When doing "the pelvic thing," have the individual stand up with their toes even and their hands hanging loosely at their side. While facing them, place your hands on each of their pelvic bones. Command the pelvic to rotate into proper position and stay there. Command the vertebrae and discs to go into proper position and be healed. Command the muscles, ligaments, tendons, and nerves to relax and go into proper position. Command the hips to be level, and all the pressure on the nerves to leave and not return in Jesus' name. Command the pelvic area to be healed in the name of Jesus.

If we can, we need to prepare ourselves before praying for the sick. Sometimes it is a "spur of the moment" event and you don't have time to prepare yourself before going to pray for the sick. But most of the time, you will know in advance that you will be praying for people. Prepare yourself by making sure you are cleansed from sin and claim knowledge, wisdom and grace on how to pray for the sick.

Spend some time reading and meditating on the Word in the areas of faith and healing. Do some praying and seeking God. Claim the anointing, glory and power to heal and deliver the sick when you minister to them. Cover yourself with the blood of Jesus and be ready to use the name of

Jesus against the sickness. Make a decision to enjoy praying for the sick and ask God to use you in this ministry.

Read and meditate in the Word of God on scriptures about the laying on of hands until you build faith in your heart. Then, take your faith, your anointing and the Word, and begin to lay hands on the sick. Remember that God wants to use you to meet the needs of sick people.

Steps for Laying Hands on the Sick:
1. Make sure you are cleansed from sin and standing on the Word of God in the name of Jesus.
2. Lay hands on the sick person by the power of the Holy Spirit and in the name of Jesus.
3. Pray, bind, loose, and command the end results to take place.
4. Believe it is done in Jesus' name by faith.
5. Thank, praise and worship God for the victory.

Chapter 15

Healing Through the Gifts of Healing(s)

But the manifestation of the Spirit is given to every man to profit withal.
For to one is given by the Spirit the word of wisdom; to another the word of knowledge by the same Spirit;
To another faith by the same Spirit; to another the gifts of healing by the same Spirit;
To another the working of miracles; to another prophecy; to another discerning of spirits; to another divers kinds of tongues; to another the interpretation of tongues.

I Corinthians 12:7-10

I Corinthians 12:28
And God hath set some in the church, first apostles, secondarily prophets, thirdly teachers, after that miracles, then gifts of healings, helps, governments, diversities of tongues.

Acts 2:4
And they were all filled with the Holy Ghost,
and began to speak with other tongues, as the
Spirit gave them utterance.

Luke 11:11-13
If a son shall ask bread of any of you that is a
father, will he give him a stone? or if he ask a
fish, will he for a fish give him a serpent?
Or if he shall ask an egg, will he offer him a
scorpion?
If ye then, being evil, know how to give good
gifts unto your children: how much more shall
your heavenly Father give the Holy Spirit to
them that ask him?

Receiving healing through the nine gifts of the Spirit is an area in the Body of Christ where there is a lot of misunderstanding. We hear about different Christians walking around with the Gifts of Healing(s) in operation, and some think that they can heal anybody who is sick anytime that they want to heal them. But unfortunately we can't control the gifts of the Spirit 100 percent of the time. We can pray, read and meditate on the Word of God. We can wait on God so the gifts of the Spirit will manifest themselves through us as often as possible. But God makes the final decision as to whether or not the Gifts of Healing(s) will manifest themselves through you to heal someone.

We can't walk around healing everyone, whether it's in a service where the Word of God has been preached and taught, or ministering one-on-one to those who need healing. The Gifts of Healing(s) are controlled by the Holy Spirit and not by man. We need to yield to the gift when it is in operation, but very seldom is everyone healed in a large meeting with the Gifts of Healing(s). Other methods of healing the sick will have to be used along with the Gifts of Healing(s).

Have you ever heard someone say, "if they can heal the sick, why don't they go to the hospitals and heal all the patients in there." This statement is a sign that the person making it doesn't know anything about the Gifts of Healing(s). God heals the sick through man but man doesn't control all the timing and results in this area. God works with a person's heart. He knows what is in their heart and what decisions they have made. Most of the time God will not override a person's will and force healing on them. At the very least, the sick person should try to arrive at a neutral state in their faith so that the Gifts of Healing(s) can work for them.

There is one thing about the Gifts of Healing(s) that is peculiar, yet unique to this gift. At times, the sick only have to be in the area where the gift is in operation to be healed. Sometimes, it doesn't take any faith at all to receive your healing--you only have to be where the Gifts of Healing(s) are flowing. Often, however, the sick will have to do something to keep their healing after they are healed by this gift. They will need to read and study the Word of God on the subject of faith and healing, in order to resist the devil if he tries to bring the sickness back on them.

There are nine gifts of the Spirit mentioned in I Corinthians 12:8-10. These nine gifts are supposed to meet the needs of the Body of Christ and are also used to draw others into the Kingdom of God. If the gifts are operating through you, they will meet the needs of others. You can't operate the Gifts of Healing(s) on yourself. You will have to receive your healing through someone else's gift or you will have to believe God for your healing by faith. The gifts operate in the Body of Christ through you to meet the needs of others.

Three of these nine gifts are revelation gifts: the word of wisdom, the word of knowledge, and the discerning of spirits. There are also three power gifts: the gift of faith, the working of miracles, and the gifts of healing(s). Finally, there are three utterance or inspirational gifts: prophecy, divers kinds of tongues, and the interpretation of tongues. All nine of these are gifts of the Spirit, and they are supernatural gifts that God gives to the Body of Christ to meet the needs of His people. We will discuss the different ways to be healed through some of these gifts.

First, we are going to discuss healing through the Word of Knowledge. The Word of Knowledge is a supernatural importation of facts--either present tense or something that has happened in the past. It is a supernatural revelation by the Holy Spirit concerning certain facts that are present or past tense in the mind of God. The Word of Knowledge can also be used to reveal sickness and demon possession in someone.

The following are some of the ways the Word of Knowledge can manifest itself through us: prophecy, tongues and interpretation, visions, dreams, inward revelation (words dropped into your mind), inward voice, audible voice, a symptom in your body (pain, but not your pain), and prayer. If someone received a Word of Knowledge concerning a sickness in your body, they would tell you about the sickness and this would build up your faith to receive healing. Then they would pray for you and you would be healed.

The Word of Knowledge would show you what sickness is causing the problem, and then, you would pray and take the name of Jesus and drive it out. I would like to remind you again, that the sick person could always reject the gifts of the Spirit, including the Word of Knowledge, if they wanted to.

If you would like the Word of Knowledge operating through you, spend time in the Word, in praying, in seeking God and believing for this gift by asking your Father for it. Keep praying and seeking God until the gift begins to operate through you.

The Discerning of Spirits is another gift of the Spirit that is needed to get some people healed. As we have already discussed, when you are praying for the sick, about 25 percent of them will need to have demon spirits cast out of them. Jesus said in John 10:10 that anything that steals, kills or destroys comes from the devil. With the gift of the Discerning of Spirits in operation, the Holy Spirit will show you what kind of spirit is behind the sickness. The Discerning of Spirits can come by visions, dreams, word of wisdom, prophecy, tongues and interpretation, an audible voice, or a word of knowledge.

When you operate in the gift of the Discerning of Spirits, you will actually see the spirit. It can be a good spirit or a bad spirit. You could see demons, angels, Jesus, Satan, seraphims, cherubims, or archangels. You will need to know how to test spirits in order to understand where they are coming from (I John 4:1-3). Make sure you take the name of Jesus and cast out the spirit that is behind the sickness when the gift of the Discerning of Spirits is in operation.

You can discern a spirit with the Word of God and by the Holy Spirit, but this is not the gift of the Discerning of Spirits. With the gift of the Discerning of Spirits you will always see the spirit. Most of the time you will usually just discern the spirit and not have the gift in operation where you will actually see the spirit. When you discern the spirit behind the sickness, deal with it the same way you would if you had actually seen it in the spirit realm. You should still take the name of Jesus and cast it out.

The Gifts of Healing(s) is the main gift of the Spirit given to the Body of Christ to receive healing from sickness. Even though most healings in the Body of Christ do not come through the Gifts of Healing(s), nevertheless, when they are in operation, it is an easy way to receive healing from any sickness. We need to understand that most healings that take place in the Church come through healing methods other than the Gifts of Healing(s). If you are sick, make sure you are not waiting for the Gifts of Healing(s) to operate on your behalf to receive healing. You should begin to believe God for your healing by faith based on other methods in His Word.

The Gifts of Healing(s) are for the supernatural healing of sickness and disease without any natural means from any source. In his book entitled, "Questions and Answers on Spiritual Gifts," Howard Carter said, "The Gifts of Healing are those healings which God effects by His Spirit. They are not to be confused with any human abilities or works, however praiseworthy. This composite gift is therefore, a spiritual and supernatural manifestation of the Holy Ghost given to the Church for the purpose of removing sickness, disease, and infirmity."

The Gifts of Healing(s) can come through one or more of the following: the laying on of hands, the spoken word, through prayer cloths, anointing with oil, the prayer of agreement, the prayer of binding and loosing, intercessory prayer, the word of knowledge, the word of wisdom, the discerning of spirits, and the gift of faith.

We can seek the Gifts of Healing(s) through prayer, reading and meditating on the Word, fasting, seeking and waiting on God. Remember that the gift will work through you as you yield to the Holy Spirit, but you can't control it 100 percent of the time. All the gifts of the Spirit are supernatural, and God controls them. We are only yielded vessels used by Him to meet the needs of the people.

Steps for Operating in the Gifts of the Spirit:

1. Read and meditate on the Word, pray, fast, and claim the gifts of the Spirit in your life and ministry.
2. Spend as much time as you can before the throne of God and in His presence each day.
3. Ask the Holy Spirit to lead and guide you in this ministry.
4. Spend as much time as you can praying in other tongues each day.
5. Be bold and speak forth whatever the Holy Spirit gives you. Don't worry about making a mistake.
6. Spend time thanking, praising and worshiping God each day.

Chapter 16

Healing Through Special Anointings

But if the Spirit of him that raised up Jesus from the dead dwell in you, he that raised up Christ from the dead shall also quicken your mortal bodies by his Spirit that dwelleth in you.

Romans 8:11

I John 2:27
But the anointing which ye have received of him abideth in you, and ye need not that any man teach you: but as the same anointing teacheth you of all things, and is truth, and is no lie, and even as it hath taught you, ye shall abide in him.

There are many ministries and certain Christians who have been given a special anointing to heal the sick. Some have a special anointing to heal certain types of sicknesses and diseases. The sickness that some individuals have a very strong anointing to pray for, and for which they have a very high success rate in getting others healed, is usually the area where they were sick and God healed them. For example, if a person has been healed of cancer, they will often have a strong faith and anointing to pray for those with cancer.

Marilyn Hickey has a strong anointing in the area of warts and growths on your body. I have heard her say that many people are healed instantaneously when she prays for them for any type of wart or growth. Ernest Angley always has a strong anointing to pray for people who have any kind of hearing problem. Kenneth Hagin said he always has a strong anointing to pray for the healing of hernias and growths.

Everyone who prays for the sick will usually have a stronger anointing to pray for certain kinds of sicknesses. Some reasons for this are that we have a stronger faith in some areas because of our Word level, and also some may have more interest in certain areas of sickness. This will motivate us to study the Word in the areas in which we are interested. As we study the Word, the knowledge we gain will increase our faith and this faith will increase our anointing, and the anointing will heal the sick.

If you think about it, you will realize that most people who pray for the sick will not even pray for someone who is totally blind. Why is this happening in the Body of Christ? It is because the individual praying for the blind person doesn't have the faith or the anointing to pray for someone's sight. In such a case, they will not even pray for the blind unless they have to. We need to pray, read and meditate on the Word of God until we have faith in our hearts, and then the anointing to pray for the blind will manifest in our ministry.

In the New Testament, we find that Jesus did not perform any healings or miracles until after John the Baptist baptized him in the Jordan River. When John baptized Jesus, the Spirit of God then came upon Him. Jesus then fasted for 40 days and nights. After this took place, He began to perform miracles and healings. Jesus performed these miracles and healings by the power or anointing of the Holy Spirit (Luke 4:14-19). We can also increase our anointing by fasting and praying. The more time we spend waiting on God, the stronger the anointing will be in our lives.

In Acts 10:38 the Word says that Jesus was anointed "with the Holy Ghost and power, and He went about doing good and healing all that were oppressed of the devil." The biggest difference between Jesus and us praying for the sick is that Jesus had the Spirit without measure (John 3:34), and we have the Spirit with measure (I Corinthians 12:11). Jesus didn't heal the sick as the Son of God during His three and one-half year ministry. He healed the sick as the Son of Man anointed by the Holy Spirit. This is the same anointing and power of the Holy Spirit that believers use to heal and deliver the sick when we pray for them today.

When we were born again or saved (this took place when we invited Jesus into our hearts to be our Lord and

Savior), the Holy Spirit came into our hearts and our spirits were recreated. We instantly became new creatures in Christ Jesus (II Corinthians 5:17). The Holy Spirit has lived inside of us ever since that event took place. In I John 2:20-27 the Word informs us that we are anointed with the power of the Holy Spirit. The Holy Spirit dwells in us, and he will quicken or heal our mortal (physical) bodies (Romans 8:9-11). Jesus said in John 7:38, "out of his (your) belly shall flow rivers of living water." The Holy Spirit will flow out of us and heal the sick if we will release our faith.

Each Christian has an anointing of the Holy Spirit. In some areas we will have a stronger anointing than others. You have to admit, if you pray for the sick, there are certain sicknesses that you are not excited about praying for. Then, there are sicknesses that you have a very strong faith and anointing to pray for, and you love to pray for healing in these areas. Normally, these are the areas where you will have the quickest and greatest results.

John 14:16-17
16 And I will pray the Father, and he shall give you another Comforter, that he may abide with you for ever.
17 Even the Spirit of truth; whom the world cannot receive, because it seeth him not, neither knoweth him: but ye know him; for he dwelleth with you, and shall be in you.

II Corinthians 1:21-22

21 Now he which stablisheth us with you in Christ, and hath anointed us, is God. 22 Who hath also sealed us, and given the earnest of the Spirit in our hearts.

We have the power or anointing of the Holy Spirit living inside of us. This anointing is released out of us with our mouth and through the touch of our hands. Jesus spoke words and told Lazarus to come forth out of the grave, and then he came out. When Jesus touched the woman who had a spirit of infirmity for 18 years and could not straighten up, she was made straight and healed in Luke 13:11-17. We need to spend time before God's throne praying and waiting on Him to increase our anointing. This will bring greater results when we speak words of faith and lay hands on the sick. If you would like to start praying for the sick, ask God to send some sick people across your path so you can pray for them.

Remember that we can minister to the sick with the Word of God by faith, and with the anointing of the Holy Spirit. We can also minister by faith, with a special anointing of the Holy Spirit. Whichever anointing you have when you are ministering to the sick, learn how to flow in it, and have a good time while you are praying for others.

Steps for Praying with a Special Anointing:
1. Pray and find out what kind of anointing God has given you to pray for the sick.
2. Use the method that the Holy Spirit leads you to use while praying for the sick.

3. Be bold and pray for the end results.
4. Thank, praise and worship God until you have the answer.

Chapter 17

Healing Through Communion

For I have received of the Lord that which also I delivered unto you, That the Lord Jesus the same night in which he was betrayed took bread:
And when he had given thanks, he brake it, and said, Take, eat: this is my body, which is broken for you: this do in remembrance of me.

I Corinthians 11:23-24

Luke 22:19-20
19 And he took bread, and gave thanks, and brake it, and gave unto them, saying, This is my body which is given for you: this do in remembrance of me.
20 Likewise also the cup after supper, saying, This cup is the new testament in my blood, which is shed for you.

When a Christian takes Communion, they should do so with the full knowledge and understanding of its significance. Communion, to many people, has become merely a religious observance. It actually has a much deeper meaning than that.

If you want to understand what Communion is all about, you will have to study the Word of God and pray until the Holy Spirit gives you a revelation of it. Communion has to be a personal experience between you and God. Once you have received the understanding from the Word of God, you can make a quality decision to receive all the promises you would like to have from God's Word as you partake of the Lord's Supper.

A foreshadow of the practice of Communion was the Passover lamb found in Exodus 12:3-11 and 37. God told Moses to instruct everyone in the nation of Israel to kill a lamb and sprinkle its blood on the two sides of the doorpost and on the upper doorpost of their homes. They were instructed to eat the lamb with their clothes on, their shoes on their feet, and with their walking staffs in their hands. They were also instructed to be dressed and ready to leave their homes before they ate the Passover meal.

God was getting them ready to leave Egypt after 400 years of bondage and slavery. There were 600,000 men, plus the women and children who left Egypt after partaking of the Passover (first communion), and they were all healed, strengthened, and made whole when they took the Passover.

The example from the original Passover applies to you and I because we are supposed to claim our healing and deliverance *before* we partake of Communion. Whatever your needs may be, even if it is healing from cancer, heart problems, diabetes, back problems, sinus problems, arthritis, fear, guilt, worry, finances, lupus, or weakness, you can receive your healing and deliverance at this time. Always walk behind your faith. One way of doing this is by claiming what you want from God *before* you take Communion. Then after you have finished taking Communion, continue to speak to the mountain (sickness), telling it where to go and stay until you are healed. Then thank and praise the Lord until you have received total healing.

The communion table is a symbol of Jesus' sacrifice for us. The wine represents the shed blood of Jesus (Hebrews 9:22). Every promise that God gave us in the New Covenant is sealed with the blood of Jesus. The blood of Jesus redeemed us from the curse of the law and everything that sin brought on mankind. Everything God gave us, which includes all His promises, is guaranteed and signed with the blood of Jesus. We need to claim freedom from sin (which includes repentance), sickness and poverty under the blood (wine) of Jesus. Always make sure that your "forgiver" is working very well, and that you have forgiven everyone who has done anything to you or against you in Jesus' name.

The bread taken during Communion represents healing for both our minds and bodies. According to Isaiah 53:4-5,

Jesus' sacrifice covered every area of man's existence. He bore spiritual torment for our sins, mental distress for our worries, cares, anxieties, and fears, as well as physical pain for our sicknesses and diseases. The stripes Jesus bore were for our healing. With His stripes we *were* healed. God the Father gave everything He had to redeem mankind from sin, sickness, disease, oppression, and poverty. We need to make sure that we discern the Lord Jesus' body when we take Communion and claim our healing at this time.

When we receive Communion, we are receiving His body and His blood. Every time we partake, we should examine ourselves closely according to I Corinthians 11:28-29. "But let a man examine himself, and so let him eat of that bread, and drink of that cup. For he that eateth and drinketh unworthily, eateth and drinketh damnation to himself, not discerning the Lord's body." Make sure you take full advantage of everything God has given you in Communion.

When receiving the Lord's Supper, we should be ready to partake of everything Jesus' sacrifice provided. We need to receive His blood (wine) and judge ourselves where sin is concerned. In I John 1:9 the Word says, "if we confess our sins, he is faithful and just to forgive us our sins, and to cleanse us from all unrighteousness." We need to make sure we are not carrying any strife or unforgiveness in our hearts (Mark 11:25-26). Confess these things and repent from your heart, and the blood of Jesus will cleanse you and set you free.

The bread represents the body of Jesus that was broken and bruised for us. The stripes laid on Jesus' back were for our healing. At Communion we should judge ourselves where sickness is concerned. We should not be having a pity party. Jesus was tortured and stripes (whippings) were put on His back and because this was done, by Jesus' stripes we were healed. Jesus purchased our healing at Calvary just as He purchased our salvation.

With this in mind, we say, "Lord it's not right that I should suffer from sickness and disease. I judge it now as being from Satan, and I reject it. I refuse to receive it any longer. By Jesus' stripes I am healed, whole and healthy. I partake of the sacrifice of your body, and I receive the healing that you have provided for me in Jesus' name." To receive healing and deliverance is not always automatic. You have to claim it and believe you have received it before and after Communion.

When you partake of Communion, make a point of judging yourself to the fullest extent in sin and sickness. Don't just receive it as a religious formality. Accept everything Jesus' sacrifice provided. If you don't examine yourself, you will be eating and drinking unworthily, not discerning the Lord's body. Paul wrote, "For this cause many are weak and sickly among you, and many sleep (are dead)." According to this verse, many Christians have died because they didn't claim their healing when they took Communion.

The Bible doesn't tell us that someone else has to serve the Lord's Supper (Communion) to us. In I Corinthians 11:25 and 26 it says, "... this do ye, as oft as ye drink it, in remembrance of me. For as often as ye eat this bread, and drink this cup, ye do show the Lord's death till he come." You can take Communion on your own and as often as you would like to take it. Set aside time to take Communion at home on a regular schedule. Take Communion in faith believing for deliverance and freedom from sin, sickness, bondage, disease, weakness, gluttony, and anything else that steals, kills or destroys.

TAKE COMMUNION AS OFTEN AS POSSIBLE

I Corinthians 11:23-31 (23) For I have received of the Lord that which also I delivered unto you, That the Lord Jesus the same night in which he was betrayed took bread: (24) And when he had given thanks, he brake it, and said, "Take eat: this is my body, which is broken for you: this do in remembrance of me". (25) After the same manner also he took the cup, when he had supped, saying, "This cup is the new testament in my blood: this do ye, as oft as ye drink it, in remembrance of me." (26) For as often as ye eat this bread, and drink this cup, ye do shew the Lord's death till he come. (27) Wherefore whosoever shall eat this bread, and drink this cup of the Lord, unworthily, shall be guilty of the body and blood of the Lord. (28) But let a man examine himself, and so let him eat of that bread, and drink of that cup. (29) For he that eateth and

drinketh unworthily, eateth and drinketh damnation to himself, not discerning the Lord's body. (30) For this cause many are weak and sickly among you, and many sleep (dead). (31) For if we would judge ourselves, we should not be judged.

Matthew 26:26-28 (26) And as they were eating, Jesus took bread, and blessed it, and brake it, and gave it to the disciples, and said, "Take, eat; this is my body." (27) And he took the cup, and gave thanks, and gave it to them, saying, "Drink ye all of it; (28) For this is my blood of the new testament, which is shed for many for the remission of sins."

Luke 22:19-20 (19) And he took bread, and gave thanks, and brake it, and gave unto them, saying, "This is my body which is given for you: this do in remembrance of me." (20) Likewise also the cup after supper, saying, "This cup is the new testament in my blood, which is shed for you."

Following are sample prayers to pray prior to or at the time of Communion:

Father, I examine my heart, and I judge myself according to the authority of the Word of God in Jesus' name. In areas where I have missed the mark such as strife, unforgiveness, envy, hatred, jealousy, covetousness, fear, worry, anxiety, unbelief, and in any other areas where the Holy Spirit reveals to me I need to repent--I am going to repent right now in the name of Jesus. In I John 1:9 your Word says, you are faithful and just to forgive us when we confess our sins, and to cleanse us from all unrighteousness. I thank you, Father, for cleansing me now from all sin.

Father, I (we) discern the Lord Jesus' body. By Jesus' stripes I am healed. Himself (Jesus) took my infirmities and bore my sicknesses. I receive healing from the top of my head to the tips of my toes, and from the top of my head to the tips of my fingers. Sickness, disease, pain, weakness, and confusion leave my mind and body and don't return in the name of Jesus.

Therefore, I (we) do not eat of the bread or drink of the cup unworthily, but I rightly discern the Lord's body by resisting anything that steals, kills or destroys from my life. I am free from the works of Satan--spirit, soul and body.

Now say this: "The Lord Jesus the same night in which he was betrayed took bread: And when he had given thanks, he brake it, and said, Take eat; this is my body, which is broken for you: this do in remembrance of me." **NOW TAKE AND EAT THE BREAD, WHICH REPRESENTS THE BROKEN BODY OF JESUS. AND, REMEMBER, BY JESUS' STRIPES WE WERE HEALED.**

Now say this: "After the same manner also he took the cup, when he had supped, saying, This cup is the new testament in my blood: this do ye, as oft as ye drink it, in remembrance of me." **NOW TAKE AND DRINK THE**

CUP, WHICH REPRESENTS THE SHED BLOOD OF
JESUS AND THE BLOOD COVENANT.

Father, I give you thanks for all you have provided
for me in Christ Jesus. I confess this day that I am
blessed of the Lord. This covenant I entered into at my
new birth is a covenant filled with thousands and
thousands of promises. All these promises belong to me,
because of the shed blood of Jesus. I receive these
promises right now as part of my covenant rights, and I
will continue to walk in them in the name of Jesus.

I am healed. I am redeemed. I am delivered from the
authority of darkness. By the stripes of Jesus I am
healed, whole and healthy. I am filled with God's
wisdom, knowledge, grace, love, joy, peace, and
strength. I receive my youth renewed. I receive the
mind of Christ. By Jesus' stripes I am healed.

Everything I set my hand to prospers. I am
prospering in my home and in my business. I am
prospering in my checking and saving accounts. I am
prospering in my family, job, community, country,
mind, and body. Thank you, Father, for prospering me
and my family.

I receive the anointing, power, wisdom, knowledge,
grace, ability, and freedom to receive healing,
wholeness, deliverance, victory, and strength in every
area of my life. I am a quick believer and a quick
receiver. I receive healing and health in every cell, gene,

nerve, muscle, bone, tissue, organ, and gland in my body—and in every area of my life including my spirit, soul and body. Thank you, Jesus, for healing me.

Chapter 18

How to Keep or Hold On to Your Healing

But that which ye have already hold fast till I come.

Revelation 2:25

James 4:7
Submit yourselves therefore to God. Resist the devil, and he will flee from you.

Galatians 6:9
And let us not be weary in well doing: for in due season we shall reap, if we faint not.

Nahum 1:9
...affliction shall not rise up the second time.

Most of the time when God heals you of a particular sickness or disease, you will have to do something to keep your healing. You will have to resist the sickness with the Word of God and the name of Jesus if the devil tries to bring it back on you.

Someone might ask, "why would the sickness come back on me? I thought once God healed someone they would always stay healed." This statement might sound good in the Church or somewhere else, but it is not scriptural. Jesus said in Revelation 2:25, "But that which you have already hold fast till I come." He was telling us in this scripture that anything we receive from God our Father, we will have to hold on to it if we want to keep it.

If you understood where the sickness comes from and who made you sick in the first place, it would help you to understand how Satan could put sickness back on you the second time. All sickness and disease come from the kingdom of Satan (John 10:10). You have to realize that God didn't make you sick. He doesn't put sickness on people. It is the devil that puts sickness on folks.

If Satan put the sickness on you the first time, why do you think he will not do it again if he gets the chance? You didn't resist the sickness the first time with the Word of God and the name of Jesus, and that's probably why you got sick in the first place. You may have permitted the devil to put sickness on you by being ignorant of the Word of God, or by refusing to apply what you already knew the Bible said about healing. But either way, it happened. You permitted or allowed the devil to put sickness on you.

The Bible informs us that after God heals us of a sickness, the devil will always try to bring back that sickness and put it back on us. James 4:7 is written to Christians and it tells us to submit ourselves to God and to resist the devil and then he will flee from us. This is also saying to you and I that if we don't resist the devil, he will not flee. If the devil tries to bring back his package of sickness and put it on you, resist it with the name of Jesus until it leaves.

There are always demon spirits behind all sicknesses. That doesn't mean someone is demon possessed when they are sick, but it does mean that there are demon spirits involved in the sickness. We should take the Word of God and the name of Jesus and remove the sickness from our minds and bodies. Then we need to take the Word of God, God's promises, and put them in our hearts. Memorize and meditate on the promises until they become a part of you. Until the Word of God has changed our thoughts, imaginations, and our feelings, it is not in our hearts.

If we are thinking correctly, we will have our thoughts in line with God's Word. Our thoughts will consist of what the Word has to say about our problem and not what our minds and bodies are saying. The Word, in I Peter 2:24, informs us that by Jesus' stripes we were healed 2,000 years ago, and that is what God has to say about sickness. Our bodies might be telling us something different; however, God's promise is on a higher level of authority. We need to keep our thoughts on God's Word and resist anything that is contrary to it, which includes sickness and disease.

Our imagination has to be controlled at all times if we are going to walk in faith. When the first symptom of sickness tries to return to your body, the devil will shoot a thought to your mind telling you that the sickness has returned. Your mind will begin to analyze what is happening to your body, and you could begin to see yourself in the hospital having an operation. Your imagination will continue to amplify the thought, if you let it, until you could have so many problems with the sickness that you could die. The devil can put thoughts and imaginations in our minds and so can we. We have to make sure we don't let our imaginations take control of our thinking and put us in bondage. Cast down thoughts and imaginations with the name of Jesus if they do not agree with the Word of God.

If we will control our thoughts and imaginations, our feelings will automatically be affected. Our thoughts and imaginations change our body chemistry. When we are thinking positively our body chemistry is positive. When we are thinking negatively our body chemistry is negative. Our feelings are greatly influenced by our body chemistry. Make sure your feelings are not controlling you. Your feelings have to be controlled with the Word of God. The Word has to take the place of the sickness inside of you (Proverbs 4:20-22). As the Word of God comes into your heart and mind, sickness will have to leave.

If that sickness tries to come back on you, take the Word of God and the name of Jesus and resist it until it leaves. The first sign that it is trying to come back will usually be some symptom that gradually tries to sneak back on you. If you will say no to the symptom in the name of Jesus as soon as it strikes you, it will leave right away. But if you put up with it for two hours, it might take you two hours to get rid of it. Resist any counterattack of the devil as soon as the first symptom touches your body.

In Matthew 12:43-45 Jesus tells us that when a demon is cast out of a person, he walks through dry places, seeking rest and finding none. Then he will come back to his house (your body), and when he finds it empty, swept and garnished, the demon will come back into your body and bring seven more demons with him more wicked than himself. Jesus said that this last state of the man was worse than the first. If your mind and body is empty and swept, that means it is void of the Word of God and the name of Jesus. Make sure you fill your house, which is your mind and body, with the Word of God. This will always keep the demon of sickness and disease from returning to you.

Anytime you get someone healed or delivered make sure, if you possibly can, that you give them some healing scriptures to memorize and meditate on so they can resist the sickness if it tries to come back on them. Also, I would encourage them to find and regularly attend a good Bible believing church that believes in praying for the sick and casting out demons.

Jesus healed a man who had been bedfast for 35 years and had never walked. John 5:14 says: "Afterward Jesus findeth him in the temple, and said unto him, Behold thou art made whole: sin no more, lest a worse thing come upon thee." Jesus was letting us know that if we go back into sin, the sickness God healed us from can come back a second time and be even worse the second time around. And, remember, there are sins of commission and sins of omission. Be sure to obey any prompting or instructions the Spirit of God personally gives you to repent.

Mark 4:17-19 informs us that there are five things that Satan can use to remove God's Word (faith) from our hearts, and put sickness back on us. These five things are **affliction** (a condition or cause of pain, suffering, or distress), **persecution** (to harass or oppress with ill treatment, to bother persistently), **the cares of this world**, **the deceitfulness of riches**, and **the lust of other things** (pleasures and lust of the eyes). All five of these things can remove the Word of God from our hearts. When this happens, we get our eyes on our five senses and the things of the world.

Satan will try to use these things to bring us back into bondage and put sickness back on us. We need to check ourselves constantly and make sure Satan is not using any of these five things to put the sickness back on us. Put the things of the Kingdom of God first place in your life.

We also need to make a quality decision to operate in the God kind of love (I Corinthians 13:1-8). This will enable us to keep the things of the world from robbing us of our faith. Also, the devil can't persecute and torment us if we are operating in the God kind of love.

The Bible informs us in Romans 5:5 that "the love of God is shed abroad in our hearts by the Holy Spirit." Ask

Jesus to love everyone through you with His kind of love. This will help you to walk in God's love and to love people just the way they are. Remember, that if people have to change before you can love them, you are operating in natural human love and not the God kind of love. The only way you can love some people is with God's love operating through you, because in the natural they don't have anything about them that you could love. We can love everybody just the way they are even though we may not be in agreement with what they are doing, just because Jesus said we could. We have to love them by faith and not by feelings to be operating in the God kind of love.

The devil will attack our minds and bodies every chance he gets. He will bring an old sickness back on us if we let him. Always remember that God wants you healed and healthy, but the devil wants you sick and weak. You are the deciding factor. What you permit, God will permit. What you accept, God will accept. What you resist, the kingdom of God has already resisted (Matthew 18:18). So, always take a bold, strong stand, and resist sickness and disease anytime it attacks you. Once you are healed, don't let the devil back in with his old sickness. Resist him with the Word of God and the name of Jesus!

What Will Permit Sickness to Come Back on You?
1. Sin/disobedience.
2. Strife--not operating in love (I Corinthians 13:4-8).
3. Not resisting the devil (sickness).
4. Not walking in faith (Word) (Romans 14:23,
   II Corinthians 5:7).

If You Have Lost Your Healing, Here Are Some Things You Can Do to Get It Back:
1. Repent.
2. Get up, brush yourself off and get back into God's Word.
3. Take the name of Jesus and rebuke the sickness out of your body. When the first symptom hits your body, attack it with the name of Jesus and drive it out. Speak to the mountain (sickness) and tell it where to go and where to stay until it leaves (Mark 11:23, Proverbs 18:21).
4. Make a committed decision to never allow that sickness to enter your body again (Luke 10:19).
5. Lock yourself in on God's Word forever.
6. Pray, meditate and act on the Word every day to maintain your healing and deliverance.

Steps for Keeping or Holding on to Your Healing:
1. Have chapter and verse for keeping your healing.
2. Make a decision that you will not lose your healing.
3. When the first symptom hits your mind or body, stop and resist it with the Word of God and the name of Jesus.
4. Thank, praise and worship God until every symptom leaves. The devil can't stand thanksgiving, praise and worship.

Sample prayer: I bind these symptoms from my body in Jesus' name. I refuse to accept any symptoms from sickness or disease in my mind or body. Satan, you can't put that disease _____ back on me. I will not accept it in Jesus' name. Jesus has already healed me and I will always walk in divine health. Thank you, Jesus, for healing me.

Chapter 19

HOW TO RECEIVE THE IMPOSSIBLE

And he (Jesus) said, The things which are impossible with men are possible with God.

Luke 18:27

I Thessalonians 5:17, 21
Pray without ceasing…. Prove all things; hold fast that which is good.

Luke 10:19
Behold, I give unto you power to tread on serpents and scorpions, and over all the power of the enemy: and nothing shall by any means hurt you.

Proverbs 18:21
Death and life are in the power of the tongue: and they that love it shall eat the fruit thereof.

To get the impossible healed in the Body of Christ will require the Church to change their prayer life. You have to realize that in the mind of God there is no such thing as someone being so sick or deformed that they cannot be healed. The Bible says in Luke 18:27 that nothing is impossible with God. In fact, the Word says that we were healed approximately 2,000 years ago when Jesus bore those stripes on His back for our healing (I Peter 2:24). That statement is true, but as far as many Christians are concerned, you could not prove it by the results they have had when praying for the sick. We need to go back to the Word of God and check on where we have missed it in the area of healing so we can get all the sick and deformed people healed that come to us.

There is one thing we have to be concerned about at all times. That is, whatever we have prayed for and claimed by faith from God, we have to work to receive. Receiving the answer to our petition rests on us. We are held responsible for receiving our answer. We have to make sure our "believer" is working properly, and that we are in a receiving mode until we have received 100 percent of what we are believing God for.

The Word of God informs us in Luke 10:19, "Behold, I give unto you power to tread on serpents and scorpions, and over all the power of the enemy: and nothing shall by any means hurt you." Nothing from Satan's kingdom should hurt us according to this verse. But sickness sure can hurt us at times if we don't know what to do, or if we are too lazy to act on God's Word. Jesus was talking to His 70 disciples in this verse, but there is no respect of persons with God (Romans 2:11). The Bible was written to you and I to instruct, guide and correct us in this life.

In Mark 16:15-18, believers are instructed to lay hands on the sick and we're told they shall recover. Psalm 91:10 says that no plague shall come near our dwellings. One interpretation of this verse is that our dwellings are the houses we live in or our physical bodies. According to this verse, your body should not have any sickness, disease or bondage living in it. We need to know how to remove any plague from our bodies with the Word of God, the power of the Holy Spirit, and the name of Jesus.

If our bodies or minds are not working correctly, it is our responsibility to stay in faith and believe God until they change and conform to the Word of God. Jesus said that He has given us power or authority over anything that would hurt us. If our bodies are deformed, sick or weak, we are being hurt by our adversary, the devil. Jesus says we have the power, but many of the churches say we don't have it. We have to make a decision to believe Jesus and His Word, or believe what someone else has told us that contradicts His Word.

Mark 9:14-29
And when he (Jesus) came to his disciples, he saw a great multitude about them, and the scribes questioning with them.
And straightway all the people, when they beheld him, were greatly amazed, and running to him saluted him.

And he asked the scribes, What question ye with them (disciples)?

And one of the multitude answered and said, Master, I have brought unto thee my son, which hath a dumb spirit;

And wheresoever he taketh him, he teareth him: and he foameth, and gnasheth with his teeth, and pineth away: and I spake to thy disciples that they should cast him out; and they could not.

He answereth him, and saith, O faithless generation, how long shall I be with you? How long shall I suffer you? Bring him unto me.

And they brought him unto him: and when he saw him, straightway the spirit tare him; and he fell on the ground, and wallowed foaming.

And he asked his father, How long is it ago since this came unto him? And he said, Of a child.

And ofttimes it hath cast him into the fire, and into the waters, to destroy him: but if thou canst do any thing, have compassion on us, and help us.

Jesus said unto him, If thou canst believe, all things are possible to him that believeth.

And straightway the father of the child cried out, and said with tears, Lord, I believe; help thou mine unbelief.

When Jesus saw that the people came running together, he rebuked the foul spirit, saying unto

him, Thou dumb and deaf spirit, I charge thee,
come out of him, and enter no more into him.
And the spirit cried, and rent him sore, and
came out of him: and he was as one dead;
insomuch that many said, He is dead.
But Jesus took him by the hand, and lifted him
up; and he arose.
And when he was come into the house, his
disciples asked him privately, Why could not
we cast him out?
And he said unto them, This kind can come
forth by nothing, but by prayer and fasting.

We read in these verses where the disciples could not
cast the dumb spirit out of the young boy and get him
healed. He was having a seizure, which was caused by a
deaf and dumb spirit. This young boy had been sick since
he was a child. He needed to be delivered from a deaf and
dumb spirit and to be healed from a sickness. If you notice
in verse 19, Jesus said His disciples were "faithless"
because they could not cast the spirit out of the boy and get
him healed. Then in verse 29, He said this kind of spirit
would not come out except through prayer and fasting.

The disciples had been living and ministering with Jesus
for over two years and during this time, they had slept,
eaten, walked, talked, and lived with Him continually. They
had watched Jesus heal people of every kind of sickness,
disease and infirmity known to man. The disciples also had
healed the multitudes with the anointing Jesus had passed
on to them. But even with all of this, Jesus said the

disciples had not been praying and fasting enough to have the power and anointing to cast out that demon spirit and get the boy healed! Jesus never told them they couldn't heal the boy. He simple told them they had not been praying and fasting enough to get him healed.

The same rule applies to you and I if we can't get someone healed and delivered or if we can't get ourselves healed. It usually means that we have not been praying and fasting enough. If we will pray long enough, the fasting will take care of itself, because the Holy Spirit will show us how to fast. We have to pray until we have the anointing to receive healing for ourselves and for those we are praying for.

As we move along this line of thinking, we have to realize that the Word of God is the only thing we have to believe and stand on until we receive the answer. Everything else around us will tell us we can't do this and that it will never work for us. As we concentrate on the Word and move by faith into the realm of prayer, Jesus said we could do "all things" in Mark 9:23.

The Church should be able to take any deformed child and pray for him or her and get the child healed. We should never see anyone that is too sick or bound by demon spirits that we cannot get healed and delivered. It will require a very strong commitment on our part to go before God's throne and stay there until we have the anointing and power to meet every need. Jesus spent 40 days and nights in prayer and fasting before He started His three and one-half year ministry. Even though He had never sinned, and His bloodstream was pure, He still prayed and fasted before He began to pray for healing and deliverance for the people.

Jesus never had anyone come to Him that was too sick or bound with demons for Him to heal and set free. Jesus ministered during His three and one-half year ministry with the power of the Holy Spirit, as the son of man. He did not minister as the Son of God with some power that He did not give us when He left the earth. We have the same Holy Spirit that Jesus ministered with during His earthly ministry. We were born in sin, and it takes the blood of Jesus to cleanse us of our sin. Maybe we should pray and fast at least as long as Jesus did, or even more, before we begin to pray for the needs of other people and ourselves.

We can see over in Acts 3:1-11 that the anointing in the disciples' lives had changed from what it had been earlier in the gospels. Peter and John were going up to the temple one-day at three o'clock in the afternoon. There was a lame man there at the temple entrance who had never walked. He was crippled from his mother's womb. Peter told him to rise and walk in the name of Jesus and the lame man was instantly healed.

Acts 5:12 says, "And by the hands of the apostles were many signs and wonders wrought among the people." Why could the disciples perform these great signs, wonders, healings, and deliverances in the book of Acts when they couldn't do them in Mark chapter nine? It is because all they were doing in the book of Acts was praying and

ministering the Word (Acts 6:4). The reason for their
success is that they had changed their prayer and fasting
life, and this gave them the power to get the lame man
healed.

Matthew 15:30-31
And great multitudes came unto him, having
with them those that were lame, blind, dumb,
maimed, and many others, and cast them down
at Jesus' feet; and he healed them:
Insomuch that the multitude wondered, when
they saw the dumb to speak, the maimed to be
whole, the lame to walk, and the blind to see:
and they glorified the God of Israel.

John 14:12
Verily, verily, I say unto you, He that believeth
on me, the works that I do shall he do also; and
greater works than these shall he do; because I
go unto my Father.

In Matthew 15:30-31 Jesus healed the lame, blind,
dumb, maimed, and everyone else who came to Him with
any kind of sickness. In fact, Jesus healed everyone who
ever came to Him for healing, no matter what was wrong
with them. Everyone around Him was not automatically
healed just because they were sick, but everyone who asked
Him to heal them was healed. We are instructed by Jesus to
do the works that He did during His three and one-half year
ministry, and we should be doing *greater* works than those
Jesus did according to John 14:12. If the Body of Christ

were praying like it should, we would be doing these *greater* works, which would include ministering salvation, healing and deliverance to everyone in need.

In Mark 11:23-24 Jesus said if we will believe and doubt not, we will have what we say, and we will have what we pray for. The saying and praying should line up with God's Word at all times. Proverbs 18:21 says that death and life are in the power of the tongue. When we are praying, we should be speaking life to whatever we are praying about. Once we have asked God for something, we then have to receive it with our faith.

According to Jesus in Mark 9:29, praying will move us from a faithless position to a position of faith. Praying will enable us to receive the impossible for ourselves, and also to pray for others who have impossible needs and help get them healed and delivered. In Matthew 7:7-8 the Bible instructs us to ask, seek and knock. The Amplified Bible puts it this way: "Keep on asking and it will be given you; keep on seeking and you will find: keep on knocking (reverently) and the door will be opened to you." We are the ones that have to receive the answer from God to our prayer. He is not holding the answer back from us.

The answer is already in the spirit realm before we asked for it, but we have to pull it out of the spirit realm into the natural realm where we live. If it's healing that we are asking for, then it is in our body where we need the manifestation of this healing, which is in the natural realm. We need to come before God's throne and in His presence

(Hebrews 4:16 and Acts 3:19), and spend time there until we have the answer to our need.

In I Thessalonians 5:17 we are instructed to pray without ceasing. Our prayer life should be the most important part of our day. Praying is saying, claiming, believing, receiving, and acting on our prayer until we receive the answer. Also, praying is communicating with God, and waiting on Him and listening to whatever instructions God may be giving us.

Jesus gave us a parable in Luke 18:1-8 about praying and not quitting until we have received our answer. He instructed us to always pray and not to faint. He went on talking about an unjust judge who feared not God and had no respect for man. A woman came to this unjust judge and asked him to protect or defend her against her adversary. The judge did not want to help her, but because he knew she would stay before him day and night until he moved on her behalf, he took care of her need.

Jesus said that God would answer the cry of His children even though they cried day and night unto Him, and that He would bear long with them. This gives us the impression that God can't give us the answer to our prayer until our **faith level gets strong enough to receive**. If we only have ten percent faith and it takes 90 percent faith to receive the answer, we have to keep on praying until we get to the 90 percent faith level. This parable is not talking about the prayer of faith, the prayer of agreement, nor any other particular kind of prayer. It is talking about coming before

God's throne and using all kinds of prayer until you receive your answer. Remember, anything you ask God for you have to know how to receive it.

Jesus said in Mark 9:27 that there is a kind of spirit that comes out only by praying and fasting. The Church knows very little about this kind of praying. The Body of Christ does not pray enough nor do most Christians even know how to pray correctly. The kind of praying Jesus is referring to here is where a Christian releases faith in God's Word until he has the answer. Your faith has to have prayer behind it if you have to wait any extended period of time for your answer. Most of the time, before you can receive the impossible, you have to make a change in your prayer life.

Let me make a few brief comments regarding fasting. There are three areas I will mention concerning fasting: time, food and things. If you are determined to begin to pray until you have the end results, you need to realize that it will require a lot of time. You will need to fast some quality time and use it in prayer. Also, you can fast from any kind of food and spend that time you would be eating in the Word of God and prayer. There are many "things" you can give up while fasting, from watching TV to other hobbies, for the purpose of spending that time in prayer. It will not benefit you to fast from something unless you use that time and energy reading and meditating in the Word of God and praying. If you will pray long enough, you will automatically fast some things in your life.

Praying for the impossible will require a strong commitment to prayer. I would like to list some things you can do while praying and believing for your "impossible to man but not to God" answer. Remember, you have to believe you have already received the answer to your request even while you are praying, and you will need to back your faith request with prayer until you have the answer. While you are praying you can be:

1. Rebuking the problem in the name of Jesus.
2. Resisting the sickness.
3. Claiming God's promises.
4. Meditating on the Word of God.
5. Asking for something (believing you have received).
6. Praying in tongues.
7. Confessing God's promises.
8. Seeking God's kingdom (righteousness, peace and joy).
9. Thanking God for the answer.
10. Knocking on heaven's door (Matthew 7:7-8)
11. Returning God's Word to Him.
12. Worshiping God.
13. Watching before the throne.
14. Confessing the Word of God.
15. Praising God for the answer.
16. Proclaiming the promises of God.
17. Calling those things that be not as though they were (Romans 4:17).
18. Listening to God.
19. Receiving the answer to your need.
20. Binding the problem (sickness) and casting it out of you in the name of Jesus.

21. Cursing the sickness and commanding it to leave in Jesus' name.
22. Resting before the throne of God.
23. Spending time calling Jesus your healer.
24. Claiming the power of the Holy Spirit.
25. Receiving the life and light of Jesus into every cell of your body (John 1:4).
26. Proclaiming that Jesus is the vine and you are the branch (John 15:1-6).
27. Receiving Jesus the healer in you.
28. Believing you are strong and not weak.
29. Acknowledging that the Holy Spirit is quickening your mind and body (Romans 8:11).
30. Confessing that by Jesus' stripes your body is healed.
31. Speaking the Word of God to your body, for example, "by Jesus' stripes I am healed."

Are you willing to spend the time in prayer to pull the answer out of the spirit realm into the natural realm? We need to keep reminding ourselves that the answer has to be pulled from the spirit realm into our bodies if we need healing. The instrument that we use to make this transfer is our tongue. The whole time we are praying, we need to believe we have received the answer based on God's Word. We need to draw or pull the healing or deliverance into our bodies through prayer until we are 100 percent healed. The same principle applies to those we are responsible for in prayer. We need to carry them on our faith until they have their answer.

Jesus said in Luke 18:1-8 that God bears long with His elect that cry day and night, and that He will answer them speedily. This gives us the impression that until our faith has reached the level where we can receive the answer, God waits patiently on us. If the answer to our healing is in the spirit realm, which the Word of God says it is in I Peter 2:24, then as soon as our faith reaches the level to receive the answer, our bodies will be healed; or the deformed child will be restored to normal, etc.

The only reason why we don't receive our answer is that we quit praying too soon. We should make up our minds that if it takes one hour, one day, one week, one month, or longer, we will never stop until we have the complete answer. God wants us to be strong, healthy, healed, and normal according to His Word.

I have heard well-known healing evangelist Norvel Hayes say, "I could take any deformed child in the world and get them healed." My question is if Norvel Hayes can get a deformed child healed, why can't you and I do the same thing? God is no respecter of persons according to the Bible. If one person can get someone healed, we all should be able to do it. But to accomplish this, we have to know how to pray until we get results. It takes a strong commitment of dedication, confession and prayer. We will need to pray, pray and pray until we can receive the answer from God with our faith. I recommend that you purchase Norvel Hayes' book titled, "How to Live and Not Die." Read this book five or six times, and it will build faith in your heart and give you boldness to believe for your healing. It is an outstanding book on how to receive healing.

Example confession and prayer:

By Jesus' stripes I am healed! Therefore, I forbid any sickness or disease to live in my body or even come upon it. I bind every disease germ, sickness, weakness, bondage, and anything that kills, steals, or destroys from my mind and body, and command it to die and come out of me in the name of Jesus. Body, you are the temple of the Holy Spirit, and sickness and disease cannot exist in you. I forbid any sickness, disease or weakness to operate in my body. I command it to disappear, dissolve and be gone in Jesus' name. I loose my mind and body from all sickness in the name of Jesus.

Body, I'm speaking to you! You come in line with the Word of God! I am healed from all sickness, disease and weakness. I'm delivered from growths and tumors. I have healthy and perfectly operating organs, cells, glands, _____, nerves, muscles, and tissues in my body. Everything in my brain and body is healed, healthy and strong. My body is chemically balanced and in harmony in Jesus' name. The Word of God is being formed in my body because by Jesus' stripes I am healed. I receive healing in every cell, tissue, gland, organ, nerve, bone, muscle, joint, and in every hair on my head. My body, soul, heart, mind, and every part of my being is healed, including my bloodstream.

All my bodily systems function in the perfection in which God created them to function, and I forbid any malfunction in my body in the name of Jesus. I command my immune system to be strong, healthy and healed, and to function properly at all times in the name of Jesus. I command my immune system to eradicate anything that steals, kills or destroys from my mind and body. The metabolism in my body is normal, because my body is chemically balanced and in harmony in the name of Jesus.

Father, I thank you that my body is in an electrochemically-balanced condition, and that all electrical and chemical frequencies in every cell in my body are balanced and operating properly. Every nerve, muscle, organ, gland, and cell in my body has the light and life of Jesus my Lord and Savior flowing in and through it, and this life is healing me right now (John 1:4).

Body, by Jesus' stripes you are healed. Body, you are strong, healthy and healed in Jesus' name. I command all my organs, glands and cells to be healed, and to work properly in the name of Jesus. Mind, be healed in Jesus' name. Mind and body, I command you to be chemically balanced in the name of Jesus. I command all sickness and disease to leave my mind and body and never return in the name of Jesus.

I receive the healing power of the Holy Spirit inside of me, healing and delivering my mind and body from all sickness and disease. Come into me Holy Spirit, and quicken and make alive my mind and body (Romans 8:11). My body is the temple (home) of the Holy Spirit, not sickness and disease. Thank you Holy Spirit, for healing me in Jesus' name.

Disease, you can't kill me because by Jesus' stripes I am healed. I command this sickness of _____ to come out of me and to not return. I take the power of the Holy Spirit, the name of Jesus, and I break _____'s (name the sickness) power over me. I claim my healing and deliverance in Jesus' name. I speak life to my body in the name of Jesus.

Steps for Receiving the Impossible:
1. Decide what you want from God.
2. Evaluate the commitment it will require for you to receive your answer.
3. Decide the steps you will use to reach your goal.
4. Totally commit your time and energy to confessing, praying, and acting on God's Word until you have your answer.
5. Thank, praise and worship God as much as possible.

Healing Scriptures

Genesis 20:17
Exodus 15:26
Exodus 23:25
Numbers 23:19
Deuteronomy 4:40
Deuteronomy 5:33
Deuteronomy 11:21
Deuteronomy 28:1-14
Deuteronomy 30:19-28
2 Kings 20:5
1 Chronicles 29:28
2 Chronicles 16:9
2 Chronicles 30:20
Job 5:26
Job 33:25
Job 37:23
Psalm 23:1
Psalm 30:2
Psalm 34:19
Psalm 41:3
Psalm 42:11
Psalm 67:2
Psalm 91:10-16
Psalm 103:3
Psalm 105:37
Psalm 107:20
Psalm 145:8-9

Psalm 147:3
Proverbs 3:1-2
Proverbs 4:20-22
Proverbs 9:11
Ecclesiastes 7:17
Isaiah 32:3
Isaiah 33:24
Isaiah 40:31
Isaiah 41:10
Isaiah 53:4-5
Isaiah 55:11
Isaiah 58:8
Isaiah 65:22
Jeremiah 30:17
Jeremiah 33:6
Hosea 13:14
Joel 3:10
Malachi 3:6
Malachi 4:2

Matthew 4:4
Matthew 4:23-24
Matthew 6:9-10
Matthew 7:11
Matthew 8:2-3
Matthew 8:5-17
Matthew 9:20-22

Matthew 9:27-36
Matthew 10:1
Matthew 12:15
Matthew 14:13-14
Matthew 14:35-36
Matthew 15:29-31
Matthew 18:19
Mark 5:1-43
Mark 6:53-56
Mark 7:25-37
Mark 9:17-29
Mark 11:22-26
Mark 16:15-20
Luke 4:16-21
Luke 4:33-41
Luke 6:6-10
Luke 6:17-19
Luke 13:11-17
John 1:1-14
John 5:2-9
John 9:1-7
John 10:10
John 14:12-15
John 15:7
John 16:23-24
Acts 3:1-8, 16
Acts 5:14-16
Acts 9:33-34
Acts 10:38
Acts 14:8-10

Acts 19:11-12
Romans 4:17-21
Romans 8:2
Romans 8:11
Romans 8:31-32
Romans 10:17
1 Corinthians 3:16
1 Cor. 6:19-20
Galatians 3:13-14
Ephesians 1:16-23
Ephesians 3:14-21
Ephesians 5:30
Ephesians 6:1-3
Philippians 2:8-10
Philippians 2:13
Col. 1:12-14
Col. 2:10, 15
1 Thess. 5:23
1 Timothy 6:12
2 Timothy 1:7
Philemon 1:6
Hebrews 2:14-15
Hebrews 4:14-16
Hebrews 10:23
Hebrews 10:35-36
Hebrews 11:1
Hebrews 11:6
Hebrews 12:12-13
Hebrews 13:8
James 1:17

James 4:7
James 5:14-16
1 Peter 2:24
1 John 3:8
1 John 4:4
1 John 5:4-5
1 John 5:14-15
3 John 2
Revelation 12:11

SINNER'S PRAYER
To Receive Jesus as Your Savior

Are you born again? Have you ever received Jesus as your Lord and Savior? Are you on your way to <u>heaven</u>? If the answer to these questions are no, read these scriptures and pray this prayer, agreeing in your heart.

John 3:16 says, "For God so loved the world, that he gave his only begotten Son, that whosoever believeth in him should not perish, but have everlasting life."

Romans 10:9-10, 13 says, "That if thou shalt confess with thy mouth the Lord Jesus, and shalt believe in thine heart that God hath raised him from the dead, thou shalt be saved. For with the heart man believeth unto righteousness; and with the mouth confession is made unto salvation. For whosoever shall call upon the name of the Lord shall be saved."

John 14:6 says, "Jesus saith unto him, I am the way, the truth, and the life: no man cometh unto the Father, but by me."

PRAY THIS PRAYER: Dear God in heaven, I come to you believing that Jesus Christ died on the cross for man's sins. I open my heart and invite Jesus to come in to be my personal Lord and Savior. Jesus, forgive me for all my sins and cleanse me from all unrighteousness. Teach me God's Word and fill me with the power of the Holy Spirit. Give me knowledge and wisdom, and show me how to live a victorious Christian life. I thank you, Jesus, because I am born again and saved through your shed blood on the cross at Calvary. I am on my way to heaven in the name of Jesus. Thank you, Jesus, for saving me!

Receiving the Fullness of the Holy Spirit

Acts 19:2 says, "Have ye received the Holy Ghost since ye believed?" It is important to receive this New Testament experience by making sure you are filled with the Holy Spirit. As believers, we should have the same experience with the Holy Spirit as the early Church did in the book of Acts. Acts 1:8 says, "But ye shall receive power...." We need the power of the Holy Spirit in our lives!

Mark 16:17 says, "...In my name...they shall speak with new tongues." In Luke 11:13 it says, "How much more shall your heavenly Father give the Holy Spirit to them that ask him?" Acts 2:38 tells us after we are born again, we shall receive the gift of the Holy Ghost. In Acts 2:4 the 120 believers in the Upper Room were "all filled with the Holy Ghost, and began to speak with other tongues, as the Spirit gave them utterance."

Remember, God is no respecter of persons (Romans 2:11). This means, what He has done for one person, He will do for you. Have you ever asked God to fill you with His mighty Holy Spirit? If the answer to that question is no, then pray this prayer and act on it by speaking in other tongues. No strange force will take control of you. Just open your mouth and begin to release the new sounds and words that God gives you.

PRAY THIS PRAYER: Heavenly Father, in the name of Jesus, I ask you to baptize me and fill me with the fullness of your Holy Spirit. Your Word says in Luke 11:13 that if I ask you to fill me with the Holy Spirit that you will do it. So I am asking you to fill me to overflowing with the Holy Spirit. I will use my lips, my tongue, and my vocal cords, and I will pray in other tongues as the Holy Spirit gives me the utterance. As the Holy Spirit gives me the language, I will speak. Thank you Jesus for filling me with the Holy Spirit. I have the Holy Spirit by faith, and now I am going to pray in other tongues.

Spend time each day praying in your new prayer language. This will keep you built up on your most holy faith, praying in the Holy Ghost according to Jude 20. In I Corinthians 14:4 the Word of God says, "He that speaketh in an unknown tongue edifieth himself." Make sure you edify and build up yourself by praying in other tongues every day.

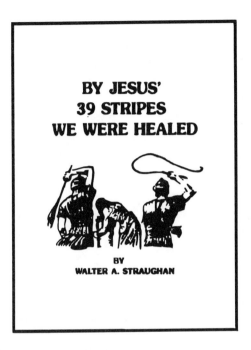

**BY JESUS'
39 STRIPES
WE WERE HEALED**

BY
WALTER A. STRAUGHAN

Healing and Deliverance Mini-Book

- Do you need physical healing?
- Do you feel down, depressed, or empty?
- Does your faith need "energizing"?
- This powerful mini-book on healing will show you how to get answers and be victorious in every area of your life! This little booklet will build your faith and minister healing to every area of your life.
- This book is the perfect size for your pocket or purse.
- It is packed with scriptures for your daily life and every need, along with guiding prayers below each verse.

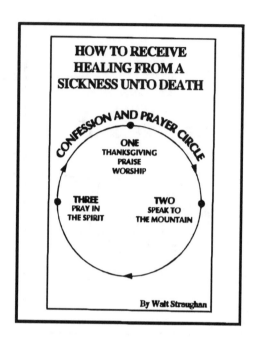

Advanced Healing and Deliverance Mini-Book

- Do you have a sickness that you haven't been able to get rid of?
- This mini-book will instruct you on how to receive healing from all diseases.
- It will show you how to release faith in God's Word continually until the sickness leaves your body.
- If you have an incurable sickness or disease, this mini-book is a must!

Walt Straughan

HOW TO RECEIVE GOD'S PROMISES

How to Receive God's Promises Mini-Book

- Would you like to know how to receive God's promises?
- Are there things you need from God's Word?
- God's promises for all your needs.
- How to possess the promises of God.
- This mini-book will show you how to bring the answer from the Word of God into your circumstances.

Walt Straughan Ministries

P.O. Box 1489
Mechanicsville, MD 20659
Phone 1-301-884-2888
Fax 1-301-884-8886
Web Page www.wsmin.org
E-mail www.wsmin@tqci.net

PRICE LIST FOR MINI-BOOKS

English Books

1. "By Jesus' 39 Stripes We Were Healed"
2. "How to Receive Healing From a Sickness Unto Death"
3. "How to Receive God's Promises"

Spanish Book-Español Libro

"Por Los 39 Latigazos De Jesus Fuimos Sanados"

Price list for all four books:

1 to 10	Contribution of:	$1.50 Each
11 to 20	20% Discount	$1.20 Each
21 to 50	40% Discount	.90 Each
51 to 100	50% Discount	.75 Each
101 and UP	56% Discount	.66 Each

All orders over $15.00 please add 10 percent for postage and handling.

You can order these books by phone, mail, web page, e-mail, or fax. Bookstores should call for a special discount.

Order More Copies of This Powerful Book Today!

P.O. Box 1489
Mechanicsville, MD 20659

Phone 1-301-884-2888
Fax 1-301-884-8886
Web Page www.wsmin.org
E-mail www.wsmin@tqci.net

BOOK ORDER PRICE LIST

English Book

"God Wants You Healed"

Eighteen Ways God Will Heal You

Price List:

1 to 3	Contribution of:	$10.00 Each
4 to 6	20% Discount	$ 8.00 Each
7 to 10	30% Discount	$ 7.00 Each
11 to 15	40% Discount	$ 6.00 Each
16 to 20	50% Discount	$ 5.00 Each

Add 15 percent to all orders for postage and handling.

You can order these books by phone, mail, web page, e-mail or fax. Bookstores should call for a special discount.

***ORDER FORM ***

	Qty.	DESCRIPTION	Total
English		**By Jesus' 39 Stripes We Were Healed**	
English		**How to Receive Healing From a Sickness Unto Death**	
English		**How to Receive God's Promises**	
Español		Por Los 39 Latigazos De Jesus Fuimos Sanados	
Tapes		8 Tapes "How to Receive Healing from a Sickness Unto Death" Sixteen One-Hour Sessions of Teaching with Outline $30.00	
Tape		One Tape "By Jesus' 39 Stripes We Were Healed" $5.00 each	
Tape		One Tape "How to Receive Healing From a Sickness Unto Death" $5.00 each	
		All orders over $15.00 please add 10 % for **Postage** and **Handling:**	
		SUBTOTAL	
English Book		**God Wants You Healed** $10.00 each or check price list	
		Add 15% to price for **Postage** and **Handling:**	
		TOTAL	

Phone Order __ E-mail__ Web Page__ Mail Order__ Fax__
Cash-Check-Money Order

Mail to: Walt Straughan Ministries

38980 F⬛⬛⬛ ⬛⬛⬛⬛⬛⬛⬛ MD 20659

⬛ Walt Straughan Ministries
59 Rosebud Lane
Staunton, VA 24401
Phone 540-337-5123 ⬛

2 Brenda need your power in God.
God give me your power
Dear God help me to be more Christ like

About the Author

Walt Straughan has been teaching on the subject of divine healing for over 20 years. He was motivated to study divine healing in 1975 after he was diagnosed with Multiple Sclerosis by his family doctor and told there was no cure for this disease. After studying the Bible, going to faith and healing seminars, and fellowshipping with Christians who prayed for the sick, he became convinced that God wanted him healed. After making a decision that he would stand on God's Word and believe Him for his healing he was healed. His healing was not instant but as he believed and confessed the Word of God over the sickness it left his body.

Mr. Straughan is a graduate from Rhema Bible School in Tulsa, Oklahoma and is a licensed minister with the Church of God. He has been conducting a weekly healing school at the National Church of God in Fort Washington, Maryland for the last seven years. While running this healing school, God has used feedback from those he has prayed for to teach and train him on how to minister healing to those who have severe sicknesses. He has seen people healed from Aids, cancer, strokes, diabetes, and almost every disease known to mankind under his ministry.

During his teaching on healing, faith and deliverance from God's Word for over the last 20 years, Walt has authored three mini-books on healing and God's promises entitled, "By Jesus' 39 Stripes We Were Healed," "How to Receive Healing From a Sickness Unto Death," and "How to Receive God's Promises.

Walt had an encounter with God as a 12-year-old boy, but he really only committed his life to God in 1975 when he was also filled with the Holy Spirit. He has been married for 42 years and has two sons and four grandchildren. He and his wife reside in Mechanicsville, Maryland.